THE *Journey* TO *Christmas*

A Daily Devotional for Advent

VICTOR MORRIS

ANM
publishers

THE *Journey* TO *Christmas*

ISBN: 978-0-9794929-6-9 Paperback

Published by:

ANM
publishers

Advancing Native Missions
P.O. Box 5303 • Charlottesville, VA 22905
www.AdvancingNativeMissions.com

Graphic Design by:
Heather Kirk, GraphicsForSuccess.com

Dedication

To our Blessed Lord and Savior,

Your First Advent was the greatest Christmas
gift ever given. Thank you!

Lord, we eagerly await Your Second Advent.
Even so, come Lord Jesus!

And to my dear Sue,

We fell in love during the holidays, and you are the
second best Christmas gift I have ever received.

I love you!

Contents

Introduction

WHAT IS ADVENT?

The song is right. Christmas: "It's the most wonderful time of the year." And I love everything about it—the lights, the greenery, the sound, the smells—all of it. But because I love it so much, I hate to see it cheapened. I must confess, it bothers me to see stores selling artificial trees in September, and commercials for "holiday sales" being broadcast before Halloween. And while hearing Christmas music played in October really doesn't bother me, knowing the reason why it's being played does. It has become a cliché to say that Christmas has become too commercialized—but it still has. We have taken something beautiful, sacred and truly full of wonder and made it tawdry.

Yet, one of the messages of the Nativity is that of hope. And I have a hope that even after decades (nay, centuries) of distorting the true meaning of Christmas we can still return it to a place of holiness. It can still inspire a hallowed awe and wonder. And it is in such hope that I offer you this book. It is my fervent desire that by taking time to reflect on the lives of Christian saints (ancient and modern), the themes of the season, and the doctrines of our faith, we can restore some of the sanctity (and sanity) of the holidays. And it is appropriate to attempt this during the somewhat forgotten observance of Advent.

We usually think of Christmas as the season from sometime around Thanksgiving until Christmas Day , or maybe even until New Year's. However, in the traditional church calendar the season before Christmas is called Advent, a word that means "coming." It was a time of expectation, looking forward to Christmas and the celebration of the birth of the Savior. The Christmas season actually begins with Christmas Day and then lasts for the 12 days afterward, ending on January 6, the feast of Epiphany.

The custom of celebrating Advent began in the church in the early 6th century. It was a tradition that began in the Western church and never did catch on in the Eastern church. In some traditions, such as the ancient Celtic church, Advent was a 40-day period before Christmas Day. However, the more common celebration observes a period of time that begins the 4th Sunday before Christmas Day and lasts through Christmas Eve.

In the traditional church calendar there were two seasons of spiritual reflection, with an emphasis on mourning and spiritual introspection. We are generally familiar with Lent, with its fasts and prayer times. Advent is very much like Lent. It is a also time of repentance, introspection, fasting and seeking God. The original idea behind Advent was that we need to prepare ourselves for Christmas. In order to appropriately celebrate the birth of Savior we needed a time to

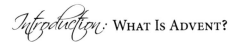

purify our hearts and cleanse our souls. In many ways, Advent (also like Lent) is a time of mourning of the soul and heart. For this reason, the traditional color of Advent is purple, lavender or dark blue, the colors of mourning in church symbolism.

However, there is also a joyful aspect to the observance, for in that era of waiting there were many prophecies and promises that God was going to send a Redeemer. So Advent is a time to meditate on the Messianic prophecies and foreshadowings of the Old Testament, and remind ourselves that God is faithful to keep all His promises. One of these is, of course, the promise of Christ's Second Coming. Just as He came the first time in fulfillment of prophecy, so He will return in fulfillment of prophecy. The coming of our Lord to establish His kingdom on this earth is also a theme of Advent.

USING THIS BOOK

Since the actual day of the week on which December 25 falls varies from year to year, then the fourth Sunday before Christmas also varies. So with this in mind, this book has been designed to include all possible days for the Advent season. The earliest possible date for the first Sunday of Advent is November 27, and that is why this devotional begins with this date. However, to use this book, all you have to do is simply count four Sundays before Christmas Day, and then go to that particular date. But we would suggest that in addition to this introduction, you also read the devotional for November 27, no matter what date the first Sunday falls on. The writing for November 27 puts the Advent and Christmas seasons in perspective.

Now, we welcome you to this journey—celebrating the first coming of the Messiah and anticipating His Second Coming.

November 27

PREPARE YE THE WAY OF THE LORD

Advent is all about anticipation, expectation and preparation. It is a time of looking forward to the birth, the coming, of the Savior.

For example, it is traditional to consider the life and ministry of John the Baptist during this time. He was the forerunner of the Messiah. According to his own words, he was the one called to prepare the way for the Lord (see John 1:23). Thus, Christ's coming was planned and prepared for by God.

So it should be with us. We should prepare and plan for our celebration of the Lord's coming. Christmas is all about remembering the Incarnation, and His birth. It is a time when, in a sense, Christ is born anew in our hearts and lives. This is something that is significant enough that it should be approached with joyful anticipation and careful preparation.

But how do you prepare for this spiritual event when you are surrounded by such gross commercialism and carnal indulgence? And isn't that what we see all about us? The pure and simple message of Christmas seems to get lost in the glitz, greed and grotesqueness of the season. Well, I think there is a solution in Advent itself. And Advent helps provide this solution in two ways.

First of all, you will recall that Advent is meant to be a time of meditation, introspection, and humility before God. Fasting and repentance are common themes in Advent devotionals. Can we not have this same focus in our daily lives? Why not turn all the busyness and frustration and irritation of preparing for Christmas into a spiritual discipline? Let me illustrate.

You are impatiently standing in line waiting and waiting and waiting for that very slow store clerk to ring up the 1000 people ahead of you. Wouldn't this be a great time to practice godly patience? What about that rude shopper who butts in line or bumps into you in the store doorway? You could see this as an opportunity to demonstrate longsuffering. What about that family member who just irritates the living daylights out of you? You dread seeing him (or her) at your family Christmas dinner. Isn't that a great chance to exhibit agape love, to go the extra mile in being loving towards the unloving and unlovable? What about all the commercialism itself? How do you handle the pollution of the Christmas message by our culture? Well, you can pray for a heart of compassion towards businessmen, Hollywood producers, store owners, marketing people, all those who so obviously need to discover the true meaning of

Christmas. They are lost souls in need of a Savior. When was the last time you prayed for their salvation?

Get the idea? Turn the irritations and frustrations that often rob us of the joy of Christmas into an exercise of godliness, an experiment in spiritual discipline.

There is also another way in which Advent can help us deal with the commercialization of this season. Recall that Advent is actually the time leading up to Christmas. It is a time of preparation for Christmas. The Christmas season only begins with Christmas Day and then continues for 12 days after that. Take advantage of that fact. Focus on Advent as a season to prepare to celebrate Christmas and all its spiritual importance. Spend time shopping and wrapping gifts for loved ones. Enjoy (or endure) office parties and family get-togethers. Put up with the increased traffic and long lines. You can take it because you know that Christmas—the real celebratory event—is on the way.

Then, when all the hustle and bustle, hurriedness and activity, pressures and stresses are all over, you can sit back and relax—and enjoy Christmas. What does it matter that all the TV specials are over? What does it matter that Christmas songs are no longer playing on the radio? You can put on your favorite Christmas CD, sit back, relax… and adore! You can rejoice for the Savior is born! And for 12 more days, while others are worrying about gift returns and presents they don't like or need, or feeling depressed because the "holidays are over"—while all this is happening for others, you are celebrating the birth of the Lord and King of the Universe.

Think of it this way: When a woman is expecting a child there is a lot to do. You have to shop. You paint and fix up the nursery. You go to baby showers. You make plans and preparations. But it is only when the baby is actually born that the real rejoicing begins. So it is with this season of the year. Advent is the shopping and preparing and planning. The celebration really starts only when the Baby is born! And that is Christmas.

November 28

SOCIALLY INITIATED NON-FRIENDLY UNAPPROVED LICENTIOUS BEHAVIOR

Ever hear about the window washer who had business cards printed that listed his job title as "Transparent Exterior Wall Maintenance Engineer"? Or what about the rather pretentious singer who announced that the next song in his Christmas concert was going to be "The Culmination Of My Personal Desires For This Natal Celebratory Season Would Be A Dyad Of Central Incisors"? Get it? He was singing "All I Want for Christmas Is My Two Front Teeth." Isn't it funny how we can take simple thing and make it so complex?

Take a look at the title of this Advent meditation. Notice the initial letters of the first six words. Putting them together yields S-I-N-F-U-L. Thus the title of this piece is really about "Sinful Behavior." Seem silly? Maybe. But it is no more silly than what we do with the reality of sin in our lives, in the human condition in general. We candy coat it. We excuse it. We justify it. We explain it away. And how often, so very often, do we blame it on someone else—parents, siblings, our spouses (shades of Adam), the devil (shades of Eve), or society in general.

I remember the horror at hearing about the Columbine shooting in 1999. Thirteen people senselessly killed at the hands of some misguided, disturbed, and (yes) very evil teenagers. My sense of outrage and sorrow over this tragedy was compounded by the way some people dealt with the event. At the time the media was tripping over themselves trying to find an explanation. It was Hollywood's fault. It was the fault of the NRA and those rabid 2nd Amendment folk. It was their parents' fault. Perhaps most commonly heard was the hindsight analysis that these two boys had been bullied, made fun of, and picked on. Here was the reason for their outrageous behavior. I distinctly remember one lady in our church almost defending the killers—she understood what it was like to be the brunt of bullies. She felt sorry for them.

I don't know about your experiences in life, but in my life I have been bullied. I have been made fun of. I have been picked on. I have experienced this in school, at work, even in church (and in case you don't know it, the church can have some really mean bullies). But you know what? I have never once considered taking an Uzi to school, work or church and blowing away all the bullies. And even if I were to do such a horrendous thing, I don't think that the actions of the bullies would in any way justify my own behavior. Simply stated, if I sin the fault lies with me and no one else. I have chosen, decided for myself, to act in this evil manner.

Now let me make one thing clear. I do not excuse or justify the bullies who picked on those young men in Columbine. Their sin is also evident. Yet their sinful and wicked behavior does not excuse or justify their victims becoming killers. In one of his writings, C. S. Lewis deals with this idea. He talks about how various factors can give us an understanding of a person's sinful behavior. But understanding does not excuse. And where there is no excuse there is no righteous justification for the action. But thankfully where we cannot excuse, we can forgive. Indeed, understanding does engender compassion. And compassion prompts forgiveness. But it still does not justify or excuse the very sinfulness of the evil act.

Scripture itself makes this point. Consider Proverbs 6:30-31: "People do not despise a thief if he steals to satisfy himself when he is starving. Yet when he is found, he must restore sevenfold. He may have to give up all the substance of his house." See the picture. We can understand a starving man taking food that does not belong to him. We can appreciate his rationale for this. We can have compassion on such a fellow. Yet, the sinfulness of the action is still there. And the consequences of sin must still be borne by this fellow. His pitiful circumstances do not absolve him of personal responsibility for his sinful acts. And they certainly would not foist the blame for his thievery on the government, his parents, the employer who had to lay him off, or his neighbor who was inconsiderate enough to still have a job.

You may be asking yourself right—why deal with such a topic in an Advent mediation. Because, dear reader, this is the heart of what Advent is all about. This preparatory season is designed to make us consider such issues. This is a season of personal introspection. In these weeks leading up to our celebration of the birth of the One who saves from sin, it is fitting that we honestly and forthrightly examine our own lives, our own hearts. We want to celebrate Messiah's birth with joy, indeed. But we also want to celebrate with purity and righteousness, and with lives and hearts that are pleasing to our blessed Savior. So to consider the exceeding sinfulness of sin is proper for this season. And to ponder my personal responsibility for my own actions is fitting and appropriate for this time.

As we have noted (in the Introduction), Advent is parallel in many ways to Lent. It is a time of reflection, spiritual examination, mourning for sin, and repentance. And this is why we approach the birth of Christ not only with joy and anticipation, but also with seriousness, spiritual sobriety, and contrition. Humility of soul and repentance in our hearts are the proper attitudes for the weeks leading up to the Christmas celebration. Then after this period of spiritual mourning and contrition, we are enabled to rejoice with undefiled spirits and pure hearts at the coming of our Lord.

A final thought: As we have stated, knowing the reasons why someone may sin does not excuse the sin. But the Good News is that what cannot be excused, can be forgiven. Now in the biblical understanding of this matter there is a great truth: We are already forgiven. This happened on the Cross. And for each of us this forgiveness can be appropriated individually and personally through God's grace. This is part of the wonder of Advent and Christmas. The Savior has come, and sin has been dealt a deathblow. For this we shout: Hallelujah!

IT'S THE LION, STUPID!

O n this date in 1898 a baby boy in Northern Ireland first saw the light of day. I wonder if his parents knew that their son was destined to become one of the premier lights of the church in the 20th century. They probably had no idea that their little Clive would grow up to become the "Apostle to the Skeptics." Yes, that auspicious day saw the advent of one of the true heroes of the Christian faith: C. S. Lewis.

I have often stated that next to the Holy Scriptures themselves the most profound influence on my thought life has definitely been C. S. Lewis. I am intrigued and amazed at both the range and depth of this man's mind. He could write on almost any topic, from science and science fiction to literary criticism and theology. And he wrote with great skill and clarity, often using plain words and short phrases that belied their apparent simplicity, for these words had the power to convey huge truths. I have read, more accurately devoured, almost everything he has written. Yet of all his works my favorites, and the ones I return to more often than any other, are his children's classics, *The Chronicles of Narnia.*

The magical appeal of Narnia has fascinated several generations of readers now. They have sold multiplied millions of copies. Several have also been made into major motion pictures. I remember when the first movie came out: *The Lion, The Witch and the Wardrobe.* It was sort of funny. LWW made tons of money for Disney and Walden Media, yet it was often treated like an unwanted stepchild. I recall that our local McDonalds had the Narnia toys in their happy meals, yet I didn't see one commercial or advertisement announcing this. At the time I was sick to death of *King Kong* commercials— the big blockbuster that year—yet I had to keep a close eye out to even catch one LWW preview. The cable channels were tripping over themselves with specials about the making of the big monkey film, but where were the background stories about the technology of the making of this other wonderful special effects movie? And the critics! Hoo, boy. They ran the gamut. Some loved the film. Ebert and Roeper gave it two thumbs up. But some almost hated it. And many were rather dismissive. (One reviewer called the acting "wooden" and stiff. Did he see the same film I did?) So, what was going on, what's the deal?

The deal was this—pure and simple—many were (and are) afraid of the obvious Christian message contained in the plot of LWW. I know what you're saying: Some don't see such a message at all. To many it is simply a children's fairy tale with some good moral overtones. (That is the reason that it is so often read and recommended in the public schools of our country.) "What Christian message?"

they say. But I think, how can anyone miss what is so obvious? Consider the climax and main focus of the story—a traitor/sinner must pay with his blood for his crime; the true King and Lord of the land, though innocent, chooses to shed his own blood in the traitor's stead; the blameless Lord is slain, but resurrects in power and glory; then the glorious King defeats the evil pretender to the throne of the land. Sound familiar? It is just as much the story of Jesus Christ, the Son of God as it is the story of Aslan, King of Narnia and Son of the Emperor-across-the-Sea. And that is what scares the bejeebers out of so many critics, reviewers, commentators and media people in this secularized, spiritually sterilized land of ours. Basically LWW and the other Narnia tales are accorded the same treatment that *The Passion of the Christ* received a couple of years ago.

However, the dismissive attitude is not confined to the secular press and non-religious media. Even some Christians seem to regard the movies as insignificant. They are viewed by these people as simplistic, childish, lacking in sophistication. Well, duh! Don't you get it? It is, after all, a children's story. The book was written for kids, and the movies were made primarily for children. Yet, that does not negate the true profundity of the stories themselves.

Yes, it is a simple story—just as the Gospel is simple. It is simple, but not simplistic. I can explain to you the basic facts of the life of Jesus and the Gospel message in one good paragraph. The story is straightforward and easy to understand. Yet, mankind has already spent two millennia trying to come to grips with this story of God become Man; the God-Man dying for the sins of the world; the God-Man rising from the dead and ascending to supernal glory and majesty in heaven. A basic, simple, uncomplicated tale—with depths of meaning that are beyond the understanding of the greatest minds of the human race. What wonder and awe flow from those two pieces of plain wood embedded in the ground outside a city called Jerusalem; what wonder and awe flow from those rough stones that form a crude table on a hillside in a place called Narnia!

And we must not forget, that is the heart of this story. The first movie, *The Lion, The Witch and the Wardrobe*, is full of funny, gentle, fantastic, stirring scenes. I love the Beavers and Tumnus. The battle scenes are powerfully done, especially for a children's film (truly dramatic, and yet bloodless to see). The animation is superb. The special effects are astonishing. The acting is natural, candid and unaffected. The film is well done in so many ways, and speaks to us on so many levels. Yet, do not ever forget that there is one, and only one, main focus of LWW, indeed of all the Chronicles of Narnia. There is one theme, one message, one focus, one heartbeat—and that is Aslan. The Lion is what it is all about.

When I hear of a Christian who has read the Chronicles of Narnia, and does not see the story and message of Christ in them, I am puzzled. No, more than puzzled... befuddled, perplexed, incredulous. I feel like crying out, "How can you not see? What is wrong with you? Don't you understand—it's **all** about Him?" Indeed, the reason that I love the Narnia tales so much is how real Aslan is, and how much I see of Christ in Aslan. When I read these books, Christ comes alive to me in a fresh and new way. Let me cite just a few examples.

I think of Lucy seeing Aslan for the first time in *Prince Caspian*. She exclaims to him that he is bigger than he was when they last met. Aslan replies to her that he is not bigger—rather, she is. He says as she grows so he will seem to get bigger. Wow—what a thought! I have experienced this in my own life. Haven't you? As we grow as believers, Jesus seems to get bigger. Yet, it is not HE that is bigger—it is simply that our understanding of His greatness has increased.

I think of the scene in *A Horse and His Boy* where two travelers meet Aslan on a dark mountainous road. The travelers are walking

November 30

THE FEAST OF ANDREW

Today is November 30, the Feast Day of Andrew the Apostle. As you will recall, Andrew was the brother of Simon Peter. Often Andrew is overshadowed by his more charismatic sibling. Yet Andrew's role in the Gospels is significant. It was Andrew who brought Peter to Christ in the first place (John 1:40-42). Andrew also brought the lad to Jesus with the lunch that was used to feed a multitude (John 6:8-9). Andrew also later brought some inquirers to Jesus (John 12:20-22). It seemed that Andrew was always bringing somebody to Jesus. What a great lesson for us! During this Advent season when we focus on the *coming* of Christ perhaps it would be wise for us to consider this question: When was the last time I helped someone *come* to Christ?

As one of the Twelve, Andrew was commissioned to carry the Gospel to all the world. Church tradition credits Andrew with evangelizing among the Scythians, thus bringing the Gospel to Central Asia and what is now southern Russia. Andrew then made his way to Greece, where he was martyred for the faith.

Legend says that he was sentenced to be crucified, but requested that he not be executed on a regular cross. Like his brother, he felt he was not worthy to die in the exact same manner as his Lord. Therefore, he was nailed to an X-shaped cross. He suffered on the cross for many days, preaching the Gospel the whole time. To this day, the Saltire or X-shaped cross is a symbol of this Apostle and Martyr.

WAYS TO CELEBRATE

To honor the memory of this hero of the faith you could make a point to do one or more of the following today:

+ Invite someone to church—to remember "Andrew the Bringer."

+ Make a point to witness to someone.

+ Make a point to witness to a family member who does not know Jesus.

+ Help provide food for a hungry person—recalling the feeding of the 5000.

+ Andrew was a fisherman, so why not have a fish dinner in his honor.

+ Pray for the harvest of souls—a great catch of men for Christ.

TILAPIA *(also called St. Peter's fish)*

Tilapia is a popular fish in restaurants today. However, it has been enjoyed since ancient times. There is a species of tilapia common in the Sea of Galilee. Tradition says it was this fish that Peter caught with two gold coins in its mouth. You may want to have tilapia for supper tonight, to commemorate Andrew and Peter, fishermen, brothers, and servants of the Messiah.

December 1

HANUKKAH

I t is likely that sometime during this Advent season it will be the
25th day of Kislev in the Hebrew calendar, which is the beginning
of the Festival of Hanukkah. (Actually it can occur as early as
November 20th, but this is rare. It is usually in December.) Have you
ever wondered what Hanukkah is all about? Let's take a moment and
review the history.

It is 165 B.C. Imagine what the ancient Jews must have been
feeling during that troubled time in the second century before
Christ. The land had been conquered almost two centuries before
by the Macedonian known as Alexander the Great. After Alexander's death there ensued a long period of foreign domination by the

Hellenistic Seleucid dynasty. During that time the sacred Temple of God had been desecrated, given over to heathen worship. One of the kings, Antiochus Epiphanes, had even sacrificed a pig on the altar of God and dedicated the Temple to the Greek god Zeus. The land itself, given to them by God, this land of their fathers, was under the dominion of this wicked heathen tyrant. Everything seemed like it was ruined, hopeless.

But then God stepped in. The Lord raised up a hero, a man of valor and courage who would no longer back down to the ungodly oppressors of his people. He was called Judah Maccabee, Judah the Hammer. He was a son of Aaron, of the priestly lineage. He had been trained by a godly father. He loved his land, his people and his God. Yet for years he had to watch as the oppressor triumphed. But now, he had had enough. He and his brothers rose up in armed resistance. They fled to the mountains and became some of history's first freedom fighters. From there they rallied the men of Israel, and fought a guerrilla campaign against the enemies of God. They inspired a generation. Finally through competent strategy, an iron will, and the help of God, the Maccabee brothers reclaimed the heritage of the Lord given to Israel. Judah Maccabee conquered Jerusalem. He ousted the alien tyrant. And he recovered the Temple of God.

But there was a major problem. The Temple had been defiled. It had been corrupted by the pollution of swine flesh and pagan ritual. Therefore the Temple had to cleansed and rededicated for the service of the Lord.

As part of the dedication process the Lamp of God had to be lighted once again. Levitical law required that the Menorah, the sacred Temple lamp, had to be kept burning. But it could only burn special holy oil. However, there was a seemingly insurmountable obstacle. There was only enough oil for one day. Just one. And

to produce new consecrated oil was a process that took days to complete. What were they to do?

The answer for Judah Maccabee and those second century B.C. Jews was to trust God and act in faith. What they did was to go ahead and consecrate the Temple. They lighted the oil lamps on the holy Menorah. And they prayed to God. And they waited.

The result? God answered with a miracle. For the lamps burned not just for one day, but for eight days. Day after day for over a week the sacred lamps burned on that one day's supply of oil. Thus, was born the Festival of Lights, the Feast of Dedication—Hanukkah.

By the way, did you know that Hanukkah is mentioned in the New Testament? Occurring in the second century before Christ, these events described are, of course, not found in the Hebrew scriptures. However, this Feast is mentioned in the Christian scriptures. Read John 10:22-40 where Jesus goes to Jerusalem at the Feast of Dedication, i.e., Hanukkah.

This is Hanukkah. A time for remembering the heroism of God's people and the miraculous provision God makes for His children. This is a time to celebrate. So spin the dreidel. Give out presents. Fry up some latkes. It is festival time.

MAKING LATKES

Eating fried foods is traditional at Hanukkah. The oil used for cooking is supposed to remind people of the oil in the miracle of the Temple's rededication. One of most common fried dishes is a potato pancake known as a latke. If you would like to try this traditional Jewish dish, on the following page, you'll find a recipe from the website AllRecipes.com.

LATKES

Ingredients

2 cups peeled and shredded potatoes

1 tablespoon grated onion

3 eggs, beaten

2 tablespoons all-purpose flour

1 1/2 teaspoons salt

1/2 cup peanut oil for frying

Directions

Place the potatoes in a cheesecloth and wring, extracting as much moisture as possible. In a medium bowl stir the potatoes, onion, eggs, flour and salt together. In a large heavy-bottomed skillet over medium-high heat, heat the oil until hot. Place large spoonfuls of the potato mixture into the hot oil, pressing down on them to form 1/4 to 1/2 inch thick patties. Brown on one side, turn and brown on the other. Let drain on paper towels. Serve hot! Makes 10-12 latkes.

December 2

TAKE HIS PEACE

The season of Advent is often such a hurried, busy time. I often think: What have we done to ourselves. We have not only robbed this time of its spiritual significance, but we have also robbed it of its joy and peacefulness. What should be a time of quiet reflection and meditation has become rushed and "care-full."

Even as I write this, I feel little peace, and lots of anxiety. I am getting ready for an upcoming event here at the office—an event I am in charge of and must plan. I am scheduled to preach in a local church on Sunday—and it is Thursday morning and right now I don't have the vaguest idea what I am going to speak on. I feel pressured by all the duties and responsibilities of my job... not to mention family, shopping, planning parties, and all the other "obli-

gations" attached to this time of the year. I am not quiet in my mind, and I am not at peace.

Yet, I should be. Advent forces us to focus on the meaning of life, the purposes of God, the promises of the Savior. One of these promises (and prophecies) is that He will be the Prince of Peace (Isaiah 9:6). He rules in peace. He grants peace. His reign is (and will ever be) a rule of peace. His future millennial kingdom is often depicted in art as the "peaceable kingdom." So, if He is the Prince of Peace, and I am His, His child, should not His peace rule in my heart. What's the problem? The problem is not with Him—it's with me. I allow things, events, people to rob me of His peace.

I remember that years ago Bill and Gloria Gaither recorded a dramatic reading set to music. It was called "Take His Peace." I have often thought of those words, especially the verb in that phrase. For there is a great truth here. If I am to have the peace of God ruling in my heart, I must choose to **take** His peace. He is the Lord of Peace (Yahweh Shalom). He offers peace. His peace is available through His grace. But I must choose to take it.

And…

I must choose to take it even if what surrounds me does not lend itself to peacefulness. Indeed, it is in such times that I MUST even more emphatically choose to take His peace.

Consider this bit of ecclesiastical trivia: In the Eastern Orthodox Church today is the feast of the prophet Habakkuk. Habakkuk understood what it was like to live in troubled times. Indeed, his book is basically focused on dialoguing with God about things the prophet doesn't understand. Yet, when we get to the conclusion of the matter, we heard some incredibly profound and powerfully moving words. Listen to the prophet:

December 2: TAKE HIS PEACE

Though the fig tree does not bud

and there are no grapes on the vines,

though the olive crop fails

and the fields produce no food,

though there are no sheep in the pen

and no cattle in the stalls,

yet I will rejoice in the LORD,

I will be joyful in God my Savior.

Habakkuk 3:17-18 NIV

Habakkuk discovered this great truth. Our focus must be on God, not circumstance. That is the way to peace—and to worship.

So in this Advent season, with all the external busyness, frustration, worry and anxiety… let us each strive internally to take and enjoy His peace. Remember, it is the free gift of the Prince of Peace Himself.

December 3

THE POWER OF WAITING

There are impatient people all over the world—of this I am sure. Yet, we Americans have a special talent for it. We do impatience extremely well. In fact, we have made it a cultural trait. We do not want to wait for anything. We want *what* we want WHEN we want it, and that means NOW! Don't ask me to wait—that's uncalled for.

But in this microwavable, instant pudding, powdered-milk, pop-up, just-add-water and poof-you-are-there society we have done ourselves great harm both psychologically and spiritually by not practicing the virtue of patience, longsuffering, endurance, perseverance, and just plain ol' waiting.

We see a wonderful illustration of the importance of waiting in Luke 2:25-40. Here we see two elderly saints of God who teach us the virtue of patience. First there is Simeon, a man who lived with a promise. He had been assured by the Holy Spirit that he would not die until he had seen the Messiah with his own eyes. Now in the twilight of his life I am sure that there were some days when he wondered if this promise was going to be fulfilled. Think about it. Waiting year after year, decade after decade—knowing God had spoken, and yet it never seemed to come true. Then one day, one wonderfully blessed day, he sees a couple enter the Temple precincts carrying a baby. The child is being brought for His dedication to the Lord.[1] His heart leaps within him. The Spirit of God in his heart cries out: "This is the One I told you about!" Immediately he recognizes that this is God's chosen One. With joyous sighs of relief, he utters words that have touched hearts through the centuries: "Now, Lord, you can let your servant depart in peace... for my eyes have seen Your salvation...." Simeon experienced his own personal epiphany (literally) because he had waited and trusted that God would do what He said He would do.

The second illustration follows immediately. There was a woman of the tribe of Asher[2] named Anna. She had experienced the joys of married life for only seven years before being widowed. After that tragic event, she spent the rest of her life as a prophetess in the Lord's house. For many, many decades she had served God with fasting and prayer. Now she comes upon the scene of Mary, Joseph, Simeon and

---

1 You may want to do some research yourself on this event. Look up the importance of Mary's purification ritual, the practice of dedicating a firstborn male child, as well as the church's celebration of Candlemas on February 2. Some interesting sidelines to the Christmas story.

2 As an aside, this is one of many Scriptures that lay to rest the false idea that there were "Ten Lost Tribes" that disappeared from the face of the earth sometime around 700 B.C. Obviously the tribe of Asher was not lost. Nor were the other nine tribes that supposedly disappeared from history.

the infant Jesus. Immediately the Spirit of God inspires her and she confirms the redemptive plan of God that would be accomplished through this divine Child. She also enters the Gospel account and becomes part of the Father's plan for His Son, because she had learned how to wait. What power there is in waiting!

Waiting is a virtue we need to rediscover in our hurried, busy, and impatient modern world. I know, waiting is no fun. None of us likes it. To be able to endure it is a discipline that must be nurtured and developed in our lives. Yet, it is the way of God. Indeed, there are so many things in God's kingdom that only come through waiting. Consider some examples:

✦ Abraham, though already age 75, with a 65-year-old wife, receives a promise of having a child. Yet he has to wait 25 years for the promise to be fulfilled.

✦ David goes through years of pursuit by Saul and what seems like endless days of running and hiding before finally becoming king of Judah, and then still waits another seven years before uniting all Israel under his authority.

✦ Daniel prays and waits for three weeks for one answer to prayer—to see God restore Israel after 70 years of oppression and captivity.

✦ Elizabeth and Zacharias have a child after many years of waiting, and it is only when they are both quite elderly that she gives birth to John, forerunner of the Messiah.

✦ Mankind itself has to pray and hope and wait for millennia before the Savior is born.

And so it goes. This is often the way God chooses to work. He teaches us to wait, to trust in Him, to take His word seriously despite the intervening circumstances, to rely on His plan and not our own.

One final thought. Consider perhaps the most famous verse dealing with waiting: Isaiah 40:31. The word for "wait" in this verse literally means to twist or braid, like twisting strands of fiber together to make a rope. The image is fascinating. Waiting on God is not meant to be just a passive, dull, irritating experience. Rather it is supposed to be a time when our lives, our hopes, our prayers, our longings are all entwined with the Lord Himself and His purposes for our lives. Waiting is an opportunity to join ourselves more closely, more intimately, with the Lord. What a shame we so often waste this wonderful opportunity by impatient and bad-tempered griping and grumbling, when we could be growing ever more interwoven into the Spirit.

This is what Advent is all about. This is what this season reminds us of. Waiting.

Lord, teach me to wait.

December 4

HAPPY THANKSGIVING

Today is the anniversary of the first Thanksgiving Day in America. It is? Yep. Although the thanksgiving celebration of the Pilgrims in Plymouth Colony has achieved popular acclaim as the first thanksgiving, the true facts of history tell us otherwise. The first settler to the New World to observe a thanksgiving service, and to commit to an annual commemoration of this practice, was in Virginia. However, not only do we see the colonists kneeling in prayer giving gratitude to God for His bringing them to the New World, it was an event that had been planned and mandated before they ever left England.

Consider the following excerpt from a newspaper article written in 1998:

"ON SEPTEMBER 16, 1619, a group of 38 English colonists headed by Captain John Woodlief sailed from England aboard the Margaret. They landed at Berkeley Hundred 10 weeks later. The settlers were sent by the London Company; it owned thousands of acres in the area, and settled and supported Berkeley Plantation.

"Exhibit A in the Virginia claim to firstness is this sentence in the company's instructions to the settlers— instructions to be opened upon reaching Virginia:

'We ordaine that the day of our ships arrivall at the place assigned for plantacon in the land of Virginia shall be yearly and perpetually kept holy as a day of thanksgiving to Almighty God.'

"These settlers held that Thanksgiving at Berkeley Hundred on December 4, 1619—a year before the Pilgrims arrived at Plymouth. Surely Woodlief and his followers were equally as grateful as the Pilgrims—equally schooled in adversity, equally determined to renew themselves with roots in the land. Surely they were equally devout and equally thankful. To suggest that they were disobedient and did not give thanks requires a superabundance of credulity and moral pretension."

> Ross Mackenzie, "The First Thanksgiving Likely Occurred Here, And Not At Plymouth," *Richmond Times Dispatch*, Nov. 26, 1998

The historical evidence indicates that indeed Woodlief did lead his band of settlers into the woods at what is now Berkeley Plantation. There they knelt and offered to God heartfelt thanks for His goodness.

They fulfilled the mandate, and honored their Lord. You'll find their pledge carved on a brick gazebo marking the location believed to be where Woodlief knelt beside the James River. Support for Virginia's claim to the first Thanksgiving came from President Bush in 2007 and before that by President Kennedy.

So "Happy Thanksgiving!"

LET US BE THANKFUL

The giving of thanks is an appropriate focus for the Advent season. This time of the year reminds us of so much for which we should be grateful—our family, friends, the church, the Word of God, the presence of the Holy Spirit, life, health, freedom, and so much more.

And think of this…

Advent is a time to remember the promises and prophecies of the coming of the Savior, the Messiah. For thousands of years men longed for a Deliverer. God had promised one would come. The first promise came just after the Fall (see Genesis 3:15). Then God repeated and confirmed His promise repeatedly. As time went by, the Lord revealed more and more details about this coming, promised Redeemer. He would be of the seed of the Woman. He would come from the family of Abraham and Isaac (see Genesis 22:18 and 26:4). He would arise as a Star from Jacob (Numbers 24:17). He would be a Ruler from the tribe of Judah (Genesis 49:10). He would be a Son of David (1 Chronicles 17:11-14, etc.)

This One who would come to free mankind from the bondage of sin, death and the devil would be a Wondrous Man indeed… the Anointed of the Lord (Psalm 2:20), the Desire of all nations (Haggai 2:7), Immanuel—God with us, born of a virgin (Isaiah 7:14), a Prophet like Moses (Deut. 18:15), the Redeemer (Isaiah 59:20), the

Root of Jesse (Isaiah 11:1), the Sun of Righteousness (Malachi 4:2)... and so much more!

So many promises. So much hope offered. Thus the promise of His coming became the longing of men. Earnestly, expectantly, with great desire they hoped and prayed for His coming and the deliverance He would bring. And for centuries, then millennia, they waited (see Hebrews 11:39-40 and 1 Peter 1:10-11).

Then, in the fullness of time (Galatians 4:4) He came! What joy! What celebration! Is that not a reason to be thankful?! Indeed, we have experienced what Abraham and Moses and David and Daniel and Isaiah only could anticipate and long for. On this side of the Manger, this side of the Cross, we know what the patriarchs and prophets could only dream about. How blessed we are.

So during this season, let us give thanks—***Messiah has come!***

December 5

DELIGHTFUL IMPRACTICALITY

"To see and delight in gifts of grace, extraordinary divine interruptions' in our ordinary lives"

I remember one morning when I had to go to the store very early. Thankfully our Harris Teeter grocery store opens at six o'clock. I pulled into the parking lot about 6:45. As I got out of the car, I looked up to see the dawn sky displayed in a delicate beauty. It was not one of those overwhelming sunrises, just a subtle yet elegant display of purples, grays, rose hues and amber tones. Just lovely. And it made me think, so many of the best things in life are beautiful—yet impractical. They serve no utilitarian purpose, but who would want to live without them?

I remember once being given a choice and wonderful gift. While we were still living in Pennsylvania, friends of ours from Virginia, Jim and Darlene Temple, sent us a beautiful e-card. It was actually a short video displaying some lovely winter scenes—leaves edged with frost, billowy snow-laden trees, and the stark beauty of ice crystals. I was fascinated. My heart was struck with a pang of utter joy. My spirits were lifted by the sheer beauty and grace of nature's wintry glory. What a delight! Thanks, Jim and Darlene.

As I reflected on these marvelous scenes, and my reaction to them, it occurred to me that some people would not appreciate such a presentation. Again there was no practical value in it. My work load was not made easier, or more efficient, by viewing these scenes, tranquil though they were. This video offered me no explanations, no advice, no plans for achieving greater success. It gave no instruction about time management, financial responsibility, or business ethics. It didn't solve the ministry concerns that I was dealing with. It filled no open positions nor were any new workers recruited. I was not inspired to work harder, smarter, or faster. I was just inspired.

Now, mind you, I have nothing against videos, tapes, books, seminars, or classes that teach you these kinds of things. I read these materials myself. I believe in hard labor, smart work and efficiency in production. As a Christian I am committed to the idea that work is a God-given gift, and a godly vocation. We are enjoined to labor on this earth, and we should do it well, and do it joyfully. Learning practical methods and techniques to do our best in life is righteous. There is virtue in practicality and efficiency.

Yet…

All that is good in life is not practical. Does a sunset give instruction in efficiency? Did God have to make rainbows so beautiful to have them fulfill their purpose? Why do babies smell so good (most of the time)—is that really necessary? We could live our productive and practical lives all day without the fragrance of a rose or the loveliness of a leaf. Life would continue its competent course in office and operating room, on the construction site or on the railroad, driving a taxi or driving a golf ball—all without such impractical things as frosted windows lacy with ice, or starlings raising a chorus of joy in the early morning sun. In some ways these things are almost unnecessary. They are definitely not practical.

These kinds of things are impractical in our work-a-day world—the world where we too often approach life only with the "bottom line" in view. They are impractical in the world of high finance and big business. Wall Street doesn't thrive on birdsong and baby smells. Madison Avenue is more concerned with glitz and sex and glamour than it is with simple things like lilac blossoms and kitten's fur. In the rarefied atmosphere of penthouses and office suites, such matters are time wasters—the desired objects of those possessed by sloth and dreams. Only fools and lazy people (and children) give heed to the smell of new mown hay or the sound of a stream tinkling in shaded luxury. Only impractical people pay attention to such unnecessary matters.

But wait, isn't that just the wonder and joy of such things! They are, indeed, unnecessary. I can make money, earn a living, and take care of myself and my family without hearing the trill of a child laughing or a seeing a brief flash of brilliance as a cardinal flies past my window. Yet, just because I don't need these brief encounters with the impractical doesn't mean they have no value. Indeed, these blatantly unnecessary things are the very experiences that sometimes encourage me to go on in life. They cause moments of such utter rapture in our mundane and necessary existences that they make life worth living.

These things are unnecessary like birthday presents are unnecessary. They are unnecessary like smiles and congratulations and surprises are unnecessary. They are gifts of grace. They are extraordinary divine interruptions in our ordinary lives. They are the warm embraces of a heavenly Father who loves each of us individually and personally, and wants to let us know it. They are love letters from a Lord who cares about our worldly, too frequently dreary existence on this planet—and Who desires to perk up our lives with epiphanies of pure delight.

I believe that such impractical matters as we are discussing here are actually some of the most valuable and precious things we possess in this life. Some people approach life with such a practical perspective that only what aids them in making money, working more efficiently, or achieving success (whatever that is) is truly valuable. But I reject such an approach to life. Worldly success and practical efficiency are not the only goals in life. They are not the only things we should strive for. There are other purposes, and I would suggest even greater purposes, to be sought after in life.

For instance, consider beauty. The seeking for, and enjoying of beauty is an end all by itself. Something that is beautiful has value just because it is beautiful. It needs nothing else to make it worthy or desirable. Beauty itself is an end in itself. Allow me to illustrate.

Suppose that you are passing through a forest in mid-January. You stop and take notice of a maple tree, starkly bare in the harsh splendor of winter. And there, at the tip of one branch, you spy a solitary leaf clinging tenaciously to the naked tree. It is a splash of dazzling red in a landscape white with snow and ice. Its leafy edge sparkles with frost. What a cheery sight on a snowy day. Now, you must understand that such an experience requires no other purpose. To see (and delight in) a lovely, delicately beautiful red maple leaf, trimmed in icy silver frost—like a sugary-edged candy sculpture—is not an experience that demands any other expectation. Its beauty is its own purpose. The joy of the moment is its own reason for being. If you take a minute out of your busyness and just enjoy the fragile beauty of such a sight, you have done all that you need to do for that moment. And for that moment, you have truly lived.

December 6

JOLLY OL' ST. NICHOLAS

Today is the feast day of Nicholas. We are all familiar with Santa Claus, and know that somehow or other St. Nicholas was transformed into Santa. But most people do not know how this happened... nor do they really know who St. Nicholas was. So let's take a moment to consider this popular, and actually little known saint.

Nicholas was born in the late third century, when Christianity was still not officially sanctioned by the Roman government. Tradition says that he was from Asia Minor. As a youth he went on a pilgrimage to the Holy Land. While returning home, a terrible storm threatened to wreck the ship he was traveling on. Yet even as a young person, Nicholas was a godly, prayerful man. He prayed for the deliverance of the ship and all aboard. The storm immediately ceased, and the ship put in at the port city of Myra. Here Nicholas was acclaimed because of the miracle of the ship and the storm. Nicholas quickly befriended the bishop of Myra, who sadly died shortly thereafter. Though only a youth and new to the city, the people of the local church decided to make Nicholas their pastor and bishop, due to his great faith and piety. Although he initially resisted, popular acclaim wouldn't let him refuse.

Nicholas came from a wealthy family, yet he did not desire to use this wealth for selfish purposes. Instead, he gave away a great deal of his riches. Usually he would try to secretly bless the people of Myra, yet it would somehow become known that he was the benefactor of so many. In fact, he became famous for his generosity. One story that illustrates his heart for giving concerns a family which had three daughters. They were a good, godly family—but they were poor. And without dowries the daughters had no hope for marriage. As one daughter after another approached marriageable age Nicholas provided each one a dowry clandestinely. He would toss a bag of gold coins through the window of the house. Some say each bag landed either in one of their shoes or in a stocking hanging near the hearth to dry. (Now you know where Santa's liking for stockings came from.)

Many fantastic miracles are credited to Nicholas. One of the most famous concerns two young boys who were traveling through the region. They came to stay at a local inn. The innkeeper was a wicked and greedy man. He robbed the boys. He then killed them, and dismembered them. He put the pieces of their bodies in a brine vat. Apparently he was planning on selling the pickled meat as though it were pork. However, God revealed the crime to Nicholas in a vision. The saintly man confronted the innkeeper, who repented and accepted Christ. Nicholas then prayed over the vat of brine, and the boys were instantly reassembled and resurrected.

Although in our modern world these fanciful legends seem to detract from taking Nicholas seriously, in the ancient and medieval world they were considered proof of the man's saintliness. For the contemporary student of church history, we can appreciate the fact that there was in fact a historical church leader named Nicholas who did lead the church in Myra. We do know that he was renowned for his generous and caring nature. We also know that he was a staunch defender of the faith. He suffered under the oppressive reign of Diocletian, and spent some time imprisoned for his beliefs. He also is reputed to have been present at the Council of Nicea in A.D. 325 where he actively and vocally defended the orthodox doctrine of the full deity of Christ. (He is also reported to have had a heated argument with the heretic Arius, and in his passion even punched Arius in the nose while on the floor of the Council. Atta boy, Nicholas!)

In the Medieval scheme of things, Nicholas became a popular and well-venerated saint. He was declared to be the patron saint of children, bankers, brewers, ships and sailors, as well as several nations—the Netherlands included. In many countries of Europe Christmas was itself a purely religious festival. However, there was still the impulse to celebrate with merriment and gift-gifting. Thus in Holland and Germany and Hungary, among other places, it was on St. Nicholas' Day (Dec. 6) that the blessed saint went about examining which children were good and which were bad, and dispensing candy and treats to the good, and burnt faggots, coal or switches to the bad. These were usually placed in the children's shoes, which they had put out on St. Nicholas Eve. (You may remember the Christmas portion of the story of Hans Brinker, in which the children place their wooden shoes on the dining room table, after having been visited by the good saint. The doors to the dining room were locked, and only opened again on the morning of Dec. 6. When the children rushed into the room, their shoes were filled to overflowing with sweet treats, trinkets, and various goodies.)

It was in America that St. Nicholas was gradually transformed into the figure we are now more familiar with. It was the Dutch of the New World settlement in New Amsterdam (now New York) who taught their children to watch for the coming of Nicholas on his feast day. They called the saint by a familiar and homely nickname: Sinter Klaas, which gradually was changed into Santa Claus. With the addition of features to his persona provided by the 19th century writings of Washington Irving and Clement C. Moore, the illustrations of Thomas Nast, and the advertising campaigns for Coca Cola (in the early 20th century), the figure of Santa Claus came to be that which we know so well today.

Admittedly much of the spirituality and true goodness of St. Nicholas has been subsumed by the modern much commercialized Santa Claus. And it is true that for far too many people, Santa himself has supplanted Jesus as the reason for the season. However, I think it is high time that the church reclaim the godly bishop of Myra. He was a kind, caring, generous, and stalwart man of faith. He was even someone who suffered persecution rather than deny the Christian message. Let us not let the world claim him as its own when he belongs to us.

One final thought about Nicholas. Although his story has been added to, fluffed up into nonsense, and even corrupted in large measure—consider this: Here was a Christian man who so exemplified the character of Christ that 1700 years later his generosity and kindness, his love of children and the less fortunate, are still legendary. What an amazing spiritual legacy he has left us. Maybe we should ask ourselves, what will our own spiritual heritage be?

December 6: Jolly Ol' St. Nicholas

Will our acts of grace and mercy be remembered 17 years from now, much less 1700?

So, kudos to you Nicholas! You were a great guy—and a true saint of God.

December 7

AMBROSE OF MILAN

Ambrose was governor of Milan during a turbulent time of history for the Roman Empire. The great controversy of the day was the nature of Christ. For years an often violent debate had raged throughout the church and empire regarding the deity of Jesus Christ. The orthodox position (that Christ was fully and completely God) had been defended by Athanasius, the bishop of Alexandria. Arius, former bishop and excommunicated heretic, held that Christ was a divine being, yet less than the Father. Arius taught that Christ was of a similar substance to God, but was not the Almighty God Himself. (Compare this with the Jehovah's Witnesses today, who are essentially modern day Arians.) The Council of Nicea in A.D. 325 had ruled in favor of Athanasius and declared the true and biblical view that Jesus was full and complete in His deity, co-equal in glory, power and divine nature with the Father and the Spirit.

In our modern times this may seem like an issue primarily for theologians—but in ancient times it divided the populace. There were actually riots and mob battles over this issue. The controversy only intensified when Constantius, son of Constantine the Great, accepted the heretical Arian view. This was the position also held by most of the Roman army—which at this time was largely made up of conquered Goths. Into this social and theological mess stepped a champion of the faith—Ambrose.

Ambrose had been governor of the northern Italian region, with Milan as the capital. When the bishop of Milan died, rioting seemed imminent. The city was almost evenly divided between the Arians and the orthodox Christians. Ambrose stepped in to quiet the populace. As he was well known and respected by both sides, he ended up being elected bishop of Milan. This election occurred on December 7, 373—the reason this day is set aside to honor this man of God.

Thus began a notable and distinguished career in the church. Ambrose consistently fought against the Arian heresy, despite pressure from the Emperor himself and the royal family. Many credit his scholarly defense of the biblical view of Christ's person as a major factor in the eventual defeat of Arianism in the West. (Some think he may even have been the author of the overtly Trinitarian Athanasian Creed.) He was noted in his time for his oratorical ability—his sermons held people enthralled. He was a prolific writer of commentaries and devotional literature. His godly influence also affected many of his parishioners, most notable among them was a young man from north Africa named Augustine. It was largely through Ambrose's influence that Augustine came to faith in Christ. Ambrose was an early and powerful influence in the developing of Augustine's spirituality and theology.

Ambrose was also noted as a writer of hymns. He is traditionally credited with composing the *Te Deum*, although this is generally not held to be true today. However, there are a number of his hymns that are still sung in churches. One of the most notable is the Christmas hymn *Veni Redemptor Gentium* or "Come, Redeemer of Nations."

Ambrose has much to teach us. However, one lesson stands out—the importance of maintaining and defending the true faith of the church. We live in a day when many consider doctrine irrelevant, old fashioned, or unnecessary. How sad. First of all, it is a tragedy that what our spiritual forefathers fought, bled, and sometimes even died for is something that we so easily neglect or even reject. However, there is a far greater tragedy. For the Scriptures themselves are plain about this matter of doctrine. If we do not believe right, then we cannot have a right relationship with God. The two things—a saving relationship with God and sound doctrine—are tied together in a bond that is eternal and unbreakable. For example, consider these verses:

+ John 17:3
+ Galatians 1:8-9
+ 2 John 9
+ 1 Timothy 4:16
+ 1 John 4:1-3
+ 2 Peter 2:1-3

During this season of Advent, as we ponder the coming of the Savior, let us remember that *Who* Jesus was is just as important as *What* He did. If He were not truly and fully Man as well as truly and fully God then our salvation has no valid basis at all. Let us thank God for men such as Ambrose... and petition our Father that He would enable us through His Holy Spirit to be as devoted to His truth, and as diligent in promoting sound doctrine, as the sainted Ambrose was in his own time. Amen.

There have been numerous translations of *Veni Redemptor Gentium.* I offer one version here:

Come, Thou Redeemer of the Earth

Veni, Redemptor Gentium, Ambrose of Milan, ca. 340-397;
translated from Latin to English by John Mason Neale, 1862.

Come, Thou Redeemer of the Earth,
And manifest Thy virgin birth:
Let every age adoring fall;
Such birth befits the God of all.

Begotten of no human will,
But of the Spirit, Thou art still
The Word of God in flesh arrayed,
The promised Fruit to man displayed.

The virgin womb that burden gained
With virgin honor all unstained;
The banners there of virtue glow;
God in His temple dwells below.

Forth from His chamber goeth He,
That royal home of purity,
A giant in twofold substance one,
Rejoicing now His course to run.

From God the Father He proceeds,
To God the Father back He speeds;
His course He runs to death and hell,
Returning on God's throne to dwell.

O equal to the Father, Thou!
Gird on Thy fleshly mantle now;
The weakness of our mortal state
With deathless might invigorate.

Thy cradle here shall glitter bright,
And darkness breathe a newer light, Where
endless faith shall shine serene,
And twilight never intervene.

O Jesu, Virgin-born, to Thee
Eternal praise and glory be,
Whom with the Father we adore
And Holy Spirit, evermore.

December 8

MARY SPEAKS

I am a Protestant. And Protestants are often put off by Mary. We usually dismiss or ignore Mary. But this is a shame, and I feel that it is really not biblical. Indeed, she is a forgotten hero of the Bible. We would do well to remember that God's own angel spoke these words to her: "Hail Mary, full of grace...." or *"Mary, you are highly favored of God."* So Mary was favored, blessed by God. We should also recall that Elizabeth declared: *"Blessed are you among all women!"* And Mary herself said, *"All generations shall call me blessed."*

It is a shame we have forgotten this, and ignored Mary, because she is a great example to us in many ways. Indeed, I think that she has much to say to us. So let's see what Mary speaks to us... what lessons we can learn from her.

First of all, she is a great example of submission to the will of God. Note her words to Gabriel: "Behold the Lord's handmaid; be it unto me according to thy word" (Luke 1:38 KJV). What does the word handmaid actually mean? In Greek it is *doule*, the feminine form of *doulos*. *Doulos* means "slave, bondman, bondslave." The word comes from a Greek word meaning "to tie, to bind." A slave was one who was under bondage—bound to the service of another. The idea is of complete submission to another's will. What rights and privileges does a slave have? None. A slave is completely under the control and domination of the master. A slave is required to do whatever the master commands. This is the picture of Mary's submission to God—absolute, total, and complete surrender to the will of God. And this was a voluntary choice on her part. What an example for us!

Another lesson we learn from Mary is that often the impossible is accomplished through the ordinary. Consider her life, her background. Mary did not come from Jerusalem, or Jericho, or Damascus, or Rome—but from Nazareth. Nazareth was a very small, insignificant town. It did not even hold a very good reputation among the people of the first century (see John 1:46). She apparently lived in poverty. Note that at the purification ceremony for the birth of Jesus, Mary offered two turtle doves (Luke 2:22-24). The usual offering for this occasion was a lamb. But an alternative of two doves was allowed for the very poor (see Leviticus 12:6-8). Thus, when Jesus was born, Mary and Joseph must have been living in great poverty. Finally, she was basically a housewife. And a Jewish housewife in the 1st century led a daily life marked by hard work and long hours.

But through this insignificant, poor, plain housewife God accomplished impossible things. Impossible? Yes. Though a virgin, in her womb was conceived the Messiah. And the One born of her womb was the very God of heaven, enrobed in flesh, incarnate in human nature. Wow! Talk about the impossible. And it occurred through the agency of this humble maid from Nazareth.

Mary also teaches us a great lesson about trusting God. Think about her reaction to the angel's words. She displayed an almost incredible confidence in God. From her response in Luke 1:38 we see in her...

+ A trust in God, no matter how hard it was to understand what was happening

+ A humble submission to the will of God

+ An acceptance of God's word on the matter

+ A submission to the Lord—to be His servant/handmaid

+ An acceptance of the greatest honor a woman could have— giving birth to the Messiah

We also see that Mary was a woman of the Word. Her faith in God, her willingness to submit, and her acceptance of God's will was rooted in her Scripturally-oriented faith. How do we know this? Well, one way we know that Mary was familiar with the Scriptures is from the *Magnificat*. This is the hymn of praise that Mary was inspired to utter when she met her cousin Elizabeth. This song is found in Luke 1:46-55. It is called *The Magnificat* from the first words, "My soul magnifies the Lord...." If you read through this hymn of praise, you will see that her hymn to God is steeped in Old Testament scripture. She was a Word-based believer.

One final lesson from this woman of faith: God always keeps His promises. Think about it. There were a number of Messianic prophecies that directly referred to Mary herself. For example, "The seed of the woman will crush the head of the serpent" (Genesis 3:15) and "A virgin shall be with child, and bear a son, who will be 'God

with us'" (Isaiah 7:14). Also, there are several Old Testament women who prefigure Mary, most notably Eve and Hannah. Furthermore, Gabriel's own prophecy to Mary about her bearing the Messiah was fulfilled in due time (Luke 1:28-37). And in addition to all this, in the life of Jesus (and Mary) there were literally hundreds of prophecies about the Messiah that were fulfilled, and in the greatest detail. In other words, God always keeps His promises. And Mary was a living example of this fact.

Think about it. Servanthood. Submission to God's will. God doing the impossible through the ordinary. Trust and confidence in God. Being grounded in the Word of God. Knowing that God will always keep His promises. All these are lessons we learn from this mighty woman of God. Yes, Mary is a true hero of the faith.

December 9

ENJOY THE JOURNEY

"Being confident of this very thing, that He who has begun a good work in you will complete it until the day of Jesus Christ." Philippians 1:6

As of today we are almost two weeks into our journey towards Christmas. Early this morning I was thinking about this fact. And it occurred to me how important Advent is—for it teaches us to wait, to anticipate, to look forward to something. In other words, it teaches us to fully appreciate and experience the process of getting somewhere.

Maybe you are like me. I am an end result, finished product kind of guy. There are some things in which I really enjoy the "doing," the "getting there." But in most things, I like to have things done. For example, decorating the Christmas tree. Decorating is fun and enjoyable. But for me the real joy is when the ornaments are on, the lights are burning, the angel is placed oh-so-carefully on top, and you dim the living room lights, sit back, and soak in the beauty, the wonder of it all. That is what I look forward to. If there were Christmas elves who would come in and decorate the tree (just the way I like it, of course) and all I had to do was enjoy the finished product, well, that would be fine by me. I like things to be finished, completed.

But life is not like that. To accomplish anything, to see any finished result there must be a process. Life is a journey. And everything we do in life is also a journey, a process. This is especially true (take note here) of the things that are most valuable in life. Indeed, can you think of one thing that really, truly matters that doesn't involve time, work, effort, a process? I don't think you can find such a thing. Marriage takes time and work, lots of love and patience and trust. A real friendship doesn't happen in a short time, it happens over years, even decades. Raising a family is not done when a baby is born, it only begins then. Establishing a ministry for God, if it is to worth its salt, will be a long journey. The things that matter are not the most immediate and instantaneous things of life.

But how slow I am to learn this. I tend to "kick against the pricks" as the Holy Spirit tries to goad me in the right direction, to trust Him for, in, and during the processes of life. And He has been working on me in this regard for a long time. (Even for Him it is a process, as I said, I am a slow learner.)

One of my early lessons came through several of the songs of Bill Gaither. Way back in 1978 he came out with an album called *Pilgrim's Progress*. (Yes, it was an album, i.e., it was a vinyl, 33 rpm LP that required, of all things, a record player!) At that time I was going through some real spiritual struggles. I definitely was not satisfied with myself. Yet, two lines from songs on that album brought me great hope and encouragement. One was this: "I am not what I want to be. I am not what I'm going to be. But, thank God, I am not what I was." Amen. It is true—God <u>has</u> worked in my life, and He <u>has</u> brought about growth and change. The second line was this: "I am learning to trust in the process that He is doing it all for my good." The one phrase that haunted me, encouraged me, and inspired me all at the same time was, "I am learning to trust in *the process….*" Wow. You mean God is not upset if I am not a finished product yet? In fact, He is involved in the journey? And I can trust the process? I can trust Him? What joy this brings!

That last sentence calls to mind another line from a song that God has also used to help me learn to trust in the process. Michael Card had an album (again, a vinyl LP—sorry this was pre-CD, folks) entitled *The Final Word.* One song on this record spoke of this very truth: "There is a joy in the journey. There is a light we can love on the way. There is a wonder and wildness to life, and freedom to those who obey." What a revelation. Not only can I learn to trust the process, but there can actually be joy in the process. The journey of life is not supposed to be one of frustration, impatient endurance, and dead end wanderings. Instead, it is a trip with the "lover of my soul." He who exists in pure peace and joy travels with me. I can have joy, freedom, even a "wildness" in my experience of the Master. What a hope! What a boost to my spirit for the miles ahead! Joy!

I think you begin to get the picture. Slowly, little by little the Spirit of God has been guiding me, teaching me, leading me in the journey. He has used people, and sermons, and Bible verses, and lessons, and songs, and a host of other vehicles to teach me this truth. However, I still remember what I think was the very first lesson about the importance of process. It was from *My Utmost For His Highest* by Oswald Chambers. I vividly remember reading the devotional lesson entitled

"After Obedience—What?" It was a revolutionary experience for me. For the first time I glimpsed God's program for my life. And His program is not a goal to strive for—rather it is a life to live. It is a process, a journey.

Let me share this devotional lesson with you, straight from the book:

July 28

AFTER OBEDIENCE - WHAT?

And straightway He constrained His disciples to get into the ship, and to go to the other side. . . ."
Mark 6:45-52

We are apt to imagine that if Jesus Christ constrains us, and we obey Him, He will lead us to great success. We must never put our dreams of success as God's purpose for us; His purpose may be exactly the opposite. We have an idea that God is leading us to a particular end, a desired goal; He is not. The question of getting to a particular end is a mere incident. What we call the process, God calls the end.

What is my dream of God's purpose? His purpose is that I depend on Him and on His power now. If I can stay in the middle of the turmoil calm and unperplexed, that is the end of the purpose of God. God is not working towards a particular finish; His end is the process—that I see Him walking on the waves, no shore in sight, no success, no goal, just the absolute certainty that it is all right because I see Him walking on the sea. It is the process, not the end, which is glorifying to God.

God's training is for now, not presently. His purpose is for this minute, not for something in the future. We have nothing to do with the afterwards of obedience; we get wrong when we think of the afterwards. What men call training and preparation, God calls the end.

God's end is to enable me to see that He can walk on the chaos of my life just now. If we have a further end in view, we do not pay sufficient attention to the immediate present: if we realize that obedience is the end, then each moment as it comes is precious.

~December 10~

A SCOTSMAN OF
PARTICULAR NOTE

December 10, 1824 saw the birth of a man whose influence is still with us today. His name was George Macdonald and he was born in Aberdeenshire, Scotland. Some of you may be already familiar with Macdonald. Many probably are not. For these latter, allow me to introduce him to you.

Macdonald was a Congregationalist minister. However, his theology was nothing less than controversial. For one thing, he rejected some basic assumptions of John Calvin. For example, he rejected the idea of Christ's death being an act of penal substitutionary atonement. He felt that to believe that God's justice was the issue in the atonement was to do a disservice to God Himself. The issue, for Macdonald, was not the wrath of God but the reality of sin itself. To him, Christ's atonement simply yet powerfully destroyed sin and its effects. In addition, he was also a universalist. He believed in hell, but he believed it was a place of temporary punishment designed by God to be used to bring sinners back to grace. Such beliefs caused him great challenges in his ministry.

So, he left the ministry. Although he served as an itinerant, sort of freelance preacher for the rest of his life, he abandoned the pastorate. His main occupation became what had been his gift and passion— writing, especially fantasy literature. His first major work, and still one of his most influential, was *Phantastes*, published in 1858. After this he became famous for his prolific fictional work, including Scottish romance novels, fairy tales, and highly imaginative fantasy novels. Some of his works include *The Princess and the Goblin*, *The Princess and Curdie*, *At the Back of the North Wind*, and *Lilith*.

These books were popular and much enjoyed during his lifetime. However, it is their abiding influence, especially among Christian authors, that has resulted in Macdonald making his mark on literature and history. Many writers credit Macdonald with having a profound effect on their thinking, their spiritual walk, and their writing. These include J.R.R. Tolkien[1], Madeleine L'Engle[2], and Lewis Carroll.[3] Noted Christian author and social commentator G. K. Chesterton was also greatly influenced by Macdonald. He said that reading *The Princess and the Goblin* "made a difference to my whole existence."

---

1   *The Hobbit* and *The Lord of Rings* are among Tolkien's work.

2   The author of *A Wrinkle In Time*, *Swiftly Tilting Planet*, and other children's fantasy literature with Christian themes.

3   Carroll wrote *Alice's Adventures in Wonderland*, and *Alice Through the Looking Glass*.

But probably the most well known person who admired Macdonald, and the one who was most greatly affected by his work, was C. S. Lewis. Lewis first read *Phantastes* when he was still an atheist. It stirred him tremendously. He said that by reading it he knew that he "had crossed a great frontier." He later would call Macdonald his literary and spiritual "master." He would even make him a prominent character in *The Great Divorce*, one of Lewis's own imaginative pieces of theological fantasy. Lewis says that reading Macdonald is what reawakened his imagination, and his soul, and started him back on a path that would eventually bring him to saving faith in Christ as Savior and Lord.

Years later Lewis would edit an anthology of Macdonald's work. In his introduction, Lewis says this about Macdonald and his influence:

> … I know hardly any other writer who seems to be closer, or more continually close, to the Spirit of Christ Himself. Hence his Christ-like union of tenderness and severity. Nowhere else outside the New Testament have I found terror and comfort so intertwined. … In making this collection I was discharging a debt of justice. I have never concealed the fact that I regarded him as my master; indeed I fancy I have never written a book in which I did not quote from him. But it has not seemed to me that those who have received my books kindly take even now sufficient notice of the affiliation. Honesty drives me to emphasize it.

We should thank God for the lasting influence of this man of God. And while we may not agree with all of his theology, we can appreciate his heart, his passion for Christ, and his lasting influence on the church and Christians, even today.

As we continue our Advent journey, perhaps you will find some thoughts from George Macdonald himself helpful in your spiritual meditations for this day:

- ✦ "Age is not all decay; it is the ripening, the swelling, of the fresh life within, that withers and bursts the husk."

- ✦ "The principal part of faith is patience."

- ✦ "It is not the cares of today, but the cares of tomorrow that weigh a man down. For the needs of today we have corresponding strength given. For the morrow we are told to trust. It is not ours yet."

- ✦ "Nothing makes one feel so strong as a call for help."

- ✦ "I find that doing of the will of God leaves me no time for disputing about His plans."

- ✦ "Friends, if we be honest with ourselves, we shall be honest with each other."

- ✦ "Division has done more to hide Christ from the view of all men than all the infidelity that has ever been spoken."

- ✦ "Afflictions are but the shadows of God's wings."

- ✦ "Do the things you know, and you shall learn the truth you need to know."

- ✦ "To have what we want is riches; but to be able to do without is power."

- ✦ "How strange this fear of death is! We are never frightened at a sunset."

- ✦ "It is the heart that is not yet sure of its God that is afraid to laugh in His presence."

December 11

"LET'S JUST GET RID OF CHRISTMAS!'

There was a time when this was the cry of a group of sincere, dedicated, very committed followers of Jesus Christ. The Puritans of 17th century England were fed up with the ungodly practices that were such an integral part of the Christian celebrations of their day. Christmas had become a time for paganesque revelry, ribaldry, drunkenness, limitless partying and blatant sacrilege. So when the Puritans came to a position of political power (regicide included) they banned and forbade Christmas. For years it was literally illegal to celebrate during this season.

This may seem radical to us today. But 'fess up. Hasn't the thought crossed your mind a time or two. Should we really keep Christmas? After all, it has become so deflated, demeaned, and devalued. It has more of the Department of Commerce about it than it does the Divinity of Christ. So I wouldn't be surprised if you have entertained this thought. It might have occurred when you saw that first Macy's Christmas commercial—on Halloween night, no less. (Aaargh!) Or the previews of that most endearing of Christmas images: A Victoria Secret's Holiday Special. (Ugh!!) Or the weariness you felt in one more school or community program advertising a "Winter Festival" or "Holiday Celebration" because for goodness sake we dare not mention the dreaded "C" word. (Sigh!!!) And if you are like many, you are ready to can the whole business if just one more person wishes you a "Happy Holidays" with such exact, precise PC intonation. (Botheration!!!!)

After all, we know that Christmas is nothing more than a racket run by a big Eastern establishment!

But this last statement gives me pause. This is what Lucy asserted in *A Charlie Brown Christmas*. That was back in the mid-60's, almost 50 years ago. The message of this timeless Peanuts classic concerns the very issue we are talking about. Is Christmas really worth keeping? Has it become too commercialized, too secularized, too paganized to even bother about. A knee-jerk reaction might be to say yes. But think about it. The world, and even more so, the church was struggling with this issue 50 years ago. Snoopy was all about Christmas glitz and glitter—winning a decorating prize was of first priority for him. Most of Charlie Brown's friends were more interested in having fun and the superficial trappings of Christmas, rather than focusing on its real meaning. Charlie Brown (along with Linus) was a lone voice in the holiday wilderness. So the tension between the true meaning of Christmas and its degradation were evident even decades ago. But let me explore this just a tad more.

I must confess. I am a Christmas nut. I have read and studied the subject for years. And in my study I have discovered an interesting fact. People have been decrying the commercialization of Christmas for generations. We just saw that in *A Charlie Brown Christmas*. But this is also true in the message of *A Miracle on 34th Street*. And I can cite you articles from as long ago as the Victorian era that complain about the true meaning of Christmas having been drowned out by other interests.

So what's the point? I think it is simply this. As with everything else in our spiritual walk, there will always be a tension between the spiritual world and this world. There will always be a magnetic drawing away from the eternal to what is temporal and carnal. This is the way of the world, the way of life on this earth. The message and meaning of Christmas has been up for grabs ever since men have been celebrating the birth of the Christ Child. Our responsibility as Christians, indeed our calling, is to handle the season and the message righteously and appropriately. And this is not done by throwing out the (Christmas) baby with the (overly-commercialized, carnal holiday) bath water. Getting rid of Christmas is not the answer. Reclaiming it, redeeming it, reorienting it—this is the answer.

Let me illustrate with words by someone who is much more eloquent and gifted with words than I could ever be. These words come from one of my favorite Christmas writings. This is a 1940 sermon by Peter Marshall called "Let's Keep Christmas." Marshall was for several years the Chaplain of the U.S. Senate before he died in 1949. Though written many decades ago, this timeless sermon still hits the nail on the head today. Consider this excerpt:

> Let's not permit the crowds and the rush to crowd Christmas out of our hearts...for that is where it belongs. Christmas is not in the stores—but in the hearts of people. Let's not give way to cynicism and

mutter that "Christmas has become commercialized. It never will be—unless you let it be. Your Christmas is not commercialized, unless you have commercialized it. Let's not succumb to the sophistication that complains: "Christmas belongs only to the children." That shows that you have never understood Christmas at all, for the older you get, the more it means, if you know what it means. Christmas, though forever young, grows old with us. Have you ever been saying, "I just can't seem to feel the Christmas spirit this year"? That's too bad. As a confession of lack of faith, it is rather significant. You are saying that you feel no joy that Jesus came into the world… You are confessing that His Presence in the world is not a reality to you…Maybe you need all the more to read the Christmas story all over again, need to sit down with the Gospel of Luke and think about it. I thank God for Christmas. Would that it lasted all year. For on Christmas Eve, and Christmas Day, all the world is a better place, and men and women are more lovable. Love itself seeps into every heart, and miracles happen. When Christmas doesn't make your heart swell up until it nearly bursts… and fill your eyes with tears…and make you all soft and warm inside…then you'll know that something inside of you is dead… So we will not "spend" Christmas…nor "observe" Christmas. We will "keep" Christmas—keep it as it is…in all the loveliness of its ancient traditions. May we keep it in our hearts, that we may be kept in its hope."

To this I say, "Amen, Brother Peter. Amen."

December 12

ONE BODY, ONE FAITH

O ne of the greatest joys of the Christian faith is the unity of the family of God. As you have read through these devotions there may have arisen a question in your mind regarding this: "Okay, so what gives?" I can hear the perplexed tone in your voice, and the frustration. "Victor, I thought you were a Protestant, so why do we keep reading about the feasts of Saints? And even more to the point, I thought you were an Evangelical! What's an Evangelical, Protestant Christian doing talking about Hanukkah and St. Ambrose and the Eastern Orthodox Church for heaven's sake?

Well, actually it is for heaven's sake!

One thing I have learned through the years—you can't box God in.[1] You can't put HIM in a little, narrow confined space and say, "This is who God is and this is what He will do. And He CAN'T do anything else." I can promise you, every time you try this, He will prove you wrong.

Isn't that part of the wonder (and joy) of the Incarnation. The Jews, especially the Pharisees and the lawyers and the rabbis had it all figured out. God gave this many laws—613 to be exact—no more, no less. According to the Talmud the Holy One (blessed be He!) was like an exalted rabbi—for example, He spends one fourth of the day studying the Talmud. He wears a Tallith (prayer shawl) and phylacteries. And He is so bound by His own laws that sometimes the rabbis could fool Him by using His own words against Him. Yep, they had God all figured out... or at least they thought so. Then, He shows up in a manger, as a baby, in human flesh. What was God doing? They just couldn't figure it out. He wasn't operating according to (their) plan. He was breaking all the rules.

And guess what? He continued to break the "rules." (Not really. They weren't His rules, they were only man-made, silly rules.) For example, He was more concerned about relieving human suffering than the legalistic observance of certain days. He was not ashamed to be seen eating with sinners and outcasts. He was confident enough in who He was that He was willing to do odd and strange things to accomplish the Father's will—like sticking his fingers in someone's ears, making mud out of dirt and spit and putting it in someone's eyes, or interrupting a funeral to raise the dead. Not normal rabbi stuff. He was the Incarnate God of the unexpected and surprising.

---

1 If you would like to undertake a good Bible study on what can happen when someone tries to "box God in" why not read 1 Kings 20:22-28. God cannot be limited in the way He sovereignly and graciously works.

December 12: One Body, One Faith

You just can't box God in!

But as I have told you I am a slow learner. So it took me a long time to learn this—especially as a Protestant, Evangelical Christian. You see, I also knew how God worked. I had it all figured out. Then I discovered a liturgical virtual saint in the person of C. S. Lewis. Oh my. Not only was he Anglican, but he was known to down a pint of ale on occasion… and he smoked too. Wouldn't seem too bad if was just a pipe. That seems homely, warm and paternal. But he also smoked cigarettes. Oh oh oh my! Then I read about some of those wacky "Catholic" saints. Like Thomas Aquinas. Here was a guy who put my prayer life to shame. And at the same time he had an intellect that just blows me away. And what about Francis of Assisi, and Ambrose, and Thomas à Kempis? Have you read *The Imitation of Christ*? If not, give it a try. A Kempis' devotion to Christ makes me feel like a spiritual kindergartener. And my, my, my… how I was inspired and challenged by Brother Lawrence and *The Practice of the Presence of God*. (I am still trying to live out the principles that Lawrence taught.) And I cannot forget Madame Guyon, a devout Catholic whose interior life puts mine to outright shame.

And that's just the Catholics… I could add some Lutherans (most notably Luther himself), and Presbyterians, and Methodists (Wesley has become one of my heroes), and even some Orthodox saints. Believe it or not, I have even developed an artistic appreciation and certain "reverence" (for want of a better word) for icons. And don't get me started on the ancient Celtic Church—Patrick and Brigid and Columba and Columbanus and David and Kevin and… well, the list goes on.

Bottom line: I know what I believe. And I hold to it dearly. You would be VERY hard pressed to sway me from the doctrines and principles I hold most closely to my heart. But I have also learned not to limit the grace of God. And I have learned that God's arms are big enough to take in all kinds of people—people I may disagree with, but I can still love as brothers and sisters.

And isn't that part of the message of this season. He came for *all* of us...

"Peace on earth, and good will to men."

December 13

SANTA LUCIA

December 13 is designated in the church calendar as a day to remember Lucy, or Lucia, a martyr for the faith. She lived in the early 4th century. She was a devout woman of God who devoted her life to Christ. When she was pledged by her parents to marry a pagan man, she refused. She gave her dowry to the poor and vowed to remain true to God. Her husband denounced her to the governor of Syracuse in Sicily. This occurred during the reign of the Roman Emperor Diocletian, a time of great persecution for the church.

Church legend records that there were several attempts to kill Lucia, but God miraculously delivered her. She was told that she was required to make an offering to the Emperor. Her reply was that she had already offered all she had to God. She said, "I offer to Him myself, let Him do with His offering as it pleases Him."

Noted for her purity, it was deemed fitting that she be humiliated by being defiled in a brothel. An ancient record of her life asserts that Lucy stated: "No one's body is polluted so as to endanger the soul if it has not pleased the mind. If you were to lift my hand to your idol and so make me offer against my will, I would still be guiltless in the sight of the true God, who judges according to the will and knows all things. If now, against my will, you cause me to be polluted, a twofold purity will be gloriously imputed to me. You cannot bend my will to your purpose; whatever you do to my body, that cannot happen to me."

Finally her eyes were taken out with a fork. For this reason she is often pictured in Christian art holding a platter with two eyes in it. Then a sword was plunged into her body. Or, some say, a dagger was plunged into her throat. She died on December 13, which became her feast day.

Lucy is honored in the Roman, Lutheran and Orthodox churches. Her feast is especially celebrated in Scandinavian countries. On the morning of December 13, a young girl will wear a crown of lighted candles. She will go from room to room awakening the family. They will arise to sing and celebrate the memory of this popular saint.

Because Lucia's feast day is one week after that of Nicholas of Myra, the two have been linked by some people. Indeed, there have been some who have said that the name of Santa Claus' wife is actually Lucy.

It is interesting that Lucia's name is Latin and means "light." A fitting name for this great heroine of the faith who boldly let the light of Christ shine through her life. She serves as an inspiration to us. Like Lucia, we should offer ourselves wholly to the Lord for His service, living in purity and holiness before Him. And we should

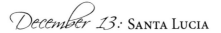

do this no matter what the cost to us personally. Nothing is more important in our lives than full, whole-hearted devotion to the Lord.

Finally, on this day it would be appropriate to remember those who suffer for their faith today. Modern history has been one of intense oppression of the church. More Christians have been martyred for the faith in the past 100 years than in the previous 1800 years combined. Every day we have 100,000's of our brother and sisters who are suffering for being Christians. On Santa Lucia Day, what could be more fitting than to lift up these members of our global family?

Remember Hebrews 13:3.

December 14

DOROTHY L. SAYERS

On this day in 1957 English novelist, playwright, poet and essayist Dorothy L. Sayers went home to be with Christ. I first became acquainted with Sayers through her detective novels about Lord Peter Wimsey. Wimsey was a somewhat dandified English peer, yet a man who had a heart of gold and mind like a steel trap. Sayers wonderful fictional prose delightfully carried the reader through the exploits of this crime-solving, monocled, erudite member of upper British society. In other words, her stories were a hoot! My wife Sue and I both loved them.

A question perhaps rises in your mind. What's so great about a writer of mystery novels? Well, first of all she was a true Christian. However, you should also know that Sayers was not only a very devout believer in Jesus but she had a quick, ready and active intellect which she used in both presenting and defending Christian truth. Her Christian worldview came through clearly, even in her fictional work—like her mystery novels. Of course, this is not the only time this occurred. Witness the spiritual concepts found in the Father Brown series of mystery stories by Chesterton. I have learned much valuable spiritual instruction from Father Brown, and from Sayers' Lord Peter.

There is an important lesson here: God can use many different vehicles for His glory. If you are a writer then you could write "Christian literature." But instead you just might write mystery stories, or science fiction, or romance novels—and God can also speak through these genres to make His voice heard among His people. (Note: Francis Schaeffer once commented on the profound influence that the Christian romance novels of Grace Livingston Hill had had on his life.) If you are a carpenter, you could use your trade skills to build churches. But instead you just might build houses for a living, and let your creative endeavors serve as a witness to the glories of the Creator. If you are skilled in office work you could serve as a church secretary. Or you just might work a regular 9 to 5 job, and glorify Jesus through answering phones and sending out emails in the secular workplace. God can use you, and what you do, wherever you are. All jobs are holy if they are done for Him.

But, let me return to Dorothy Sayers—because I didn't mean to leave her standing in Lord Peter's London flat, like she could go nowhere else. Indeed, this lady could travel. She was an accomplished poetess. She achieved celebrity as a playwright, and was commissioned by the BBC to write a number of plays which they produced. She also was an able defender of the faith. Her theological writings can stand up against just about anybody. Consider *The Mind of the Maker*, in which she discusses the creative ability of humanity as a reflection of the *Imago Dei*, the image of God we all bear—the imprint of the Creator on our souls. She also uses this discussion to consider the intricacies of the nature of the Triune God. What a mind she had! Is it any surprise that she was a friend of the likes of C. S. Lewis and his circle?

If you have not read any of Sayers' work, why not give them a try? I think you will be glad you explored her writings.

Also consider some quotes by Dorothy Sayers:

✦ "In the world it is called Tolerance, but in hell it is called Despair, the sin that believes in nothing, cares for nothing, seeks to know nothing, interferes with nothing, enjoys nothing, hates nothing, finds purpose in nothing, lives for nothing, and remains alive because there is nothing for which it will die."

✦ "None of us feels the true love of God till we realize how wicked we are. But you can't teach people that—they have to learn by experience."

✦ "Time and trouble will tame an advanced young woman, but an advanced old woman is uncontrollable by any earthly force."

✦ "Trouble shared is trouble halved."

✦ "Those who prefer their English sloppy have only themselves to thank if the advertisement writer uses his mastery of the vocabulary and syntax to mislead their weak minds."

✦ "Except ye become as little children, except you can wake on your fiftieth birthday with the same forward-looking excitement and interest in life that you enjoyed when you were five, 'ye cannot enter the kingdom of God.' One must not only die daily, but every day we must be born again."

✦ "This recognition of the truth we get in the artist's work comes to us as a revelation of new truth. I want to be clear about that. I am not referring to the sort of patronizing recognition we give a writer by nodding our heads and observing, 'Yes, yes, very good, very true—that's just what I'm always saying.' I mean the recognition of a truth that tells us something about ourselves that we had not been always saying, something that puts a new knowledge of ourselves within our grasp. It is new, startling, and perhaps shattering, and yet it comes to us with a sense of familiarity. We did not know it before, but the moment the poet has shown it to us, we know that, somehow or other, we had always really known it."

✦ "I always have a quotation for everything—it saves original thinking."

December 15

IMPOSSIBILITIES

Today December 15, is a very important holiday. It is national "Herding Cats Day." Sorta seems appropriate that this particular observance falls during Advent. Ever feel like it is almost impossible to get it all done—that preparing for Christmas is like herding cats? The shopping, the cooking, the wrapping, the planning, the parties, etc. etc. etc. How will you get it all done?

Considering the impossible is a fitting subject for consideration at this season of the year. Think of the story of the Annunciation, that awesome experience Mary had when she was approached by none other than Gabriel himself. Remember? He told her, "You will have a Son!" Her answer: "How can this be, seeing that I have never been with a man?" Mary's reaction was natural, not unexpected.

After all, virgins do not have babies. That is pretty plain. No genius intellect required here. But take note of the angel's response to her question: "With men this is impossible, but nothing is impossible with God." Wow!

I love Mary's attitude at this juncture. She had not lost reason. She still understood basic human biology. But just as much as she knew her own physiology, she also knew her God. "I am the Lord's handmaid. May it be to me according to your word." In other words, I accept that God can do the impossible. I love Mary. What a shining example of simple (yet incredibly deep) faith and trust in God. Would that I could be more like her. "It's impossible!" I cry. "But, Lord, You go ahead and do it. You can do whatever you want. I choose to believe You."

Yep. Thinking about the impossible is a good thing at this time of the year. So why not take a break from all the madness, the rush, the things you can't handle right now? Sit back and relax. Contemplate the reality that what seems overwhelming, even impossible to us, is possible with God. He can do anything. And if He can do anything, and we are His, why do we worry.

As you are learning to get over your worries about the impossible, consider these quotes:

- ✦ "The state of faith allows no mention of impossibility." — TERTULLIAN

- ✦ "Faith, mighty faith, the promise sees and looks to God alone. Laughs at impossibilities and cries, 'It shall be done.'" — CHARLES WESLEY

- ✦ "Pray the largest prayers. You cannot think a prayer so large that God in answering it, will not wish you had made it larger. Pray not for crutches but wings." — PHILLIPS BROOKS

✦ "Your religious life is every day to be a proof that God works impossibilities; your religious life is to be a series of impossibilities made possible and actual by God's almighty power." — ANDREW MURRAY

✦ "The thing that taxes almightiness is the very thing which we as disciples of Jesus ought to believe He will do." — OSWALD CHAMBERS

✦ "I think God is to be glorified by asking the impossible of Him." — JIM ELLIOT

Want to have a laugh at the impossibilities of your day? Why not check out the commercial on "Cat Herding"? You can see it by going to YouTube and searching for "cowboys herding cats commercial." It's a riot!

December 16

LAS POSADAS

In Latin America today marks the beginning of *Las Posadas*. This is a nine day celebration that recalls the journey of Mary and Joseph and their wandering the streets looking for lodging. Celebrations may vary from country to country. As a sample, let's consider the Las Posadas traditions of Mexico.

Decorations for Las Posadas may occur many weeks before the actual celebration—as early as November 2. But on December 16 the festivities get into full swing, and are celebrated each evening until Christmas Eve. This is technically a novenario, i.e., a novena, a nine-day religious observance. The nine days is said to be based on the nine months that Madre Maria carried the Lord Jesus in her womb. The posadas is basically a dramatic reenactment of the arduous journey that Mary and Joseph undertook from Nazareth to Bethlehem. As we know, when they arrived in Bethlehem they had to search for a place to stay—thus the name of the festival: In Spanish *posada* means "lodging" or "inn."

On each evening of the festival people travel from house to house. Children dress up as angels, shepherds, Mary and Joseph. An angel leads the process. Adults follow the train of children, with candles in their hands. As they travel, they sing. Their song is a plea for lodging. Finally, the designated hosts will sing a reply, offering their home as shelter. Then a party is enjoyed, with traditional festival foods. These include hot tamales, fried cookes called *buñuelos,* and hot punch. The party comes to a climax with the breaking of a piñata shaped like a star. Each night's celebration is a *posada.* The last posada occurs on Christmas Eve, and is immediately followed by midnight Mass.

Although Las Posadas is not a traditional part of our usual observance of Advent and the period leading up to Christmas, it is worthwhile to consider the symbolic significance of this holiday festival. In fact, there are two lessons for us here. First is the fact of our own pilgrimage. And second, we should consider the place accorded Jesus in our own hearts.

In our comfortable, affluent modern lifestyles we have pretty much lost the concept of being wayfarers in this earth. Do we believe, or even truly comprehend, passages of Scripture like "our citizenship is in heaven" (Philippians 3:20), "here we have no continuing city, but we seek one to come" (Hebrews 13:14, or "Beloved, I beg you as sojourners and pilgrims, abstain from fleshly lusts which war against the soul" (1 Peter 2:11). The idea of not belonging on this earth and living for another place is, sad to say, foreign to far too many Christians today.

In the ancient Celtic church of the British Isles they propounded a unique view of martyrdom. They asserted that there were three types of martyrs: red, white and green. The red martyrs are those who actually shed their blood or give their lives for the faith, what we usually think of as martyrs. White martyrs are believers who dedicate their lives to live separate from the world in absolute consecration to spirituality. In other words, they become monks or hermits. But the third class is very unique and interesting for us. Green martyrs are those who continue live in the secular, mundane, everyday world— yet live lifestyles of utter devotion and consecration. They make their jobs and families and everyday experiences an offering and sacrifice to God. In other words, they truly live as pilgrims on this earth. They recognize and live as people who are only passing through this life. Their values, desires, goals, and purposes are directed to a different world. They are green martyrs, still on the temporal earth but living for the eternal realms.

So during this time of Las Posadas, let us recall the fact that we are pilgrims, wayfarers, sojourners on this earth.

The second lesson we learn from Las Posadas is the importance of the place we accord Jesus in our hearts. The image of Mary and Joseph, away from home, wandering the streets searching for a place to stay, a place for Mary to give birth—it definitely tugs at our hearts. It has engendered many poems, songs and sermons. And often in these creative writings the innkeeper is viewed as the villain of the story. Yet, we must ask ourselves—are we any less a villain? What do we do with Jesus in His "wanderings," His seeking for a place to reside? His desire is to dwell fully in our hearts.

Years ago I remember doing a study on Ephesians 3:17: "... that Christ may dwell in your hearts through faith." As I recall, in the original the word "dwell" here has a very rich imagery. It is the picture of someone being comfortably at home, settling down, at rest and peace in one's own house. Imagine sitting down with your feet propped up before a roaring fire, comfortable, at ease, just enjoying being at home. Get the idea? Now, let me ask you. Does Jesus feel like that in your

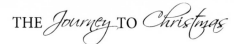

heart? That is the admonition of Ephesians 3:17. Our lives should be such that Christ can feel totally at home, completely comfortable in our hearts.

Or, are there are many other things that crowd Him out? Are there things that make Him uncomfortable? Things that He doesn't approve of, or enjoy being around? In the place that truly belongs to Him, the heart He bought and paid for, is He at home? Is He allowed to dwell comfortably there?

Gives one pause, doesn't it. It does me.

Las Posadas is a pretty good idea. It is a reminder that we are on a journey, pilgrims in this earth. It is also a reminder that Jesus was not only turned out before His birth in Bethlehem, but He is far too often turned out of His proper abode in our lives today. Maybe it would be a good idea for us to give some thought to observing Las Posadas, at least in our hearts, if no where else.

December 17

STAND UP, STAND UP
FOR JESUS

Many people shy away from the book of Revelation. Not only does it seem hard to understand, but its images of demonic locusts and dragons and wrathful angels and seas of blood are a bit much to take. But the fact is that John wasn't the only man of God to be exposed to horrific images of prophetic truth. Some 500+ years before the birth of Christ the prophet Daniel was himself seeing visions of golden images, monstrous beasts, and divine judgments. And it is to Daniel that we will looking today. In the Eastern Orthodox Church, and in some Lutheran churches, December 17 is the day to remember this mighty man of God.

We all know the story of Daniel. We learned about his being thrown to the lions when we were just children. (I wonder how many flannel board pictures of Daniel in the lions' den have been stared at by youngsters through the years.) We all have heard of his visions, his wise counsel to his conquering kings, his trust in God no matter what. And as happens with so many such biblical stories, our familiarity can lessen our appreciation for the story of this man of God.

Daniel is an amazing example of a man of faith in the public sphere. He survived exile from his native land. He came into royal favor under Nebuchadnezzar. He lasted through the fall of Babylon and its being conquered by the Medo-Persians. He again rose to prominence as a royal official under the Persian monarchy. Yet through all these changes and challenges he remained steadfast and loyal, both to his God and his earthly sovereign. Noted for his wisdom and God-given insights, he was a noted counselor and advisor who put all the supposed wise men of both the Babylonian and Persian courts to shame. Daniel demonstrates that it is possible for a person to be righteous before his God and live a godly life yet still be active in politics and public life. Would that we had more men and women like him in Washington today!

When I think of Daniel I immediately recognize his unswerving faith and trust in God, as well as his total and utter devotion to serve his Lord. Though a statesmen and civil official, he was not swayed by public opinion. His spiritual commitment would not allow him to eat foods that were unacceptable to his faith. Can you imagine a politician today going to a state dinner and refusing to eat what everyone else is eating? Can you imagine *yourself* doing it? Most of us (not just politicians) are far too worried about what other men think of what we do, rather than being concerned about what God thinks of what we do. Hard to swallow, maybe, but isn't this the truth?

And think of that incident with the lions. Can you imagine how this situation would be handled today. Suppose a modern day Christian were in Daniel's place. The spin doctors would be putting their twists on Daniel's daily devotions, trying to make his prayers appear as a cultural duty not a religious exercise. Daniel's official court handlers would be conducting polls, basing their advice to him on what the masses were saying. The king and the prophet would both be guided by the latest surveys in how they handled things. And surely Daniel could wiggle his way out of the situation. Surely he could find some way to justify changing his behavior. After all, hadn't God put him in this position of authority? Didn't God expect him to remain alive, to continue to do his job? It seems ludicrous to think that God would actually allow one of His servants to suffer. Besides, what's wrong with being secretive about your faith? It's okay to believe in God, just don't make a public issue of it.

Can't you see this happening—at least in our day?

But I just don't want to pick on today's public officials. I think that in reality we probably have the politicians in D.C. that we have because we are getting what we deserve. Indeed, the problem with our country today is not what is wrong with Washington, it is what is wrong with the church!

In this regard, I think that it is interesting to consider the prophet's very name. Daniel means "God is my judge." Daniel was not concerned about the court of popular opinion. He really wasn't even concerned about what the king thought. He was committed to His God, and God was his judge. He knew the One he ultimately had to answer to. And this is what is really important.

I sometimes wonder if Christians today live with any thought of the fact that one day they will stand before Jesus Christ at His *bema*, His judgment seat, and give an account of their lives. If we lived with this reality more present in our minds, do you think we might act and speak and think differently? Do you think we might stop making such pitiful excuses for not attending church, not praying every day, not reading our Bible, not watching those objectionable movies, not listening to music that glorifies sin, not listening to gossip, not loving our neighbor, not doing all those things that we know we should be doing? Do you think we might just quit making excuses, period?! Wouldn't that be something?

All this pondering reminds me of a song by Keith Green, "Asleep in the Light." Consider some of the lyrics:

> *"Oh bless me Lord, bless me Lord, you know it's all I ever hear,*
>
> *No one aches, no one hurts, no one even sheds one tear,*
>
> *But He cries, He weeps, He bleeds, and He cares for your needs,*
>
> *And you just lay back and keep soaking it in, oh, can't you see it's such sin?*
>
> *"The world is sleeping in the dark,*
>
> *That the church can't fight, cause it's asleep in the light,*
>
> *How can you be so dead, when you've been so well fed,*
>
> *Jesus rose from the grave, and you, you can't even get out of bed,*
>
> *Oh, Jesus rose from the dead, come on, get out of your bed."*

Lord help us.

One day we will face a king far more terrible than Darius of Persia. And we will have to give answers to Him for how we lived. Excuses will fail miserably in that day. Truly we pray, Lord help us to give a good account when we stand before God, who is my Judge.

"Asleep in the Light" by Keith Green © 1979 BMG Songs/Birdsong Music/Ears to Hear Music/ASCAP

December 18

THINK ABOUT IT...
REALLY!

I remember a few years ago when I received a book in the mail, a rather strange book. It is actually two books in one. The first is entitled *A Geocentricity Primer*, and the second is *The Geocentric Bible # 3*. Both books have one purpose, to convince thinking Christians that the earth really is the center of the universe. The author was serious about this. The accompanying cover letter informed me that this book was being sent free of charge to over 46,000 pastors throughout the United States. The reason for his zeal is pretty basic: If the Bible presents the concept of an earth-centered cosmos, and we are to trust the Bible, then this must be so. He attempts to use astronomical and physical evidences to demonstrate that it reasonable to believe that the earth is indeed the literal focus of the universe. I remember that I only glanced at his arguments, but what I saw was at least interesting. He seemed to be a compelling writer. And since he has an earned Ph.D. in astronomy, he should know something about his topic.

Now I will tell you right off that I personally do not believe that the earth is the center of the universe. I *accept* the heliocentric conception of the solar system. I *do think* that our solar system is located on one arm of this swirling spiral galaxy of ours. And I am *of the opinion* that there are billions of galaxies scattered throughout the universe, and our Milky Way is not outstanding among these, at least not from a scientific point of view. And yet, I ask myself, *how* do I know this? Think about it. I am sure that all of you believe in the usual, "normal," view of the universe. But how do you know that this view is true?

Currently we seem to be questioning almost everything. Yet, even in this postmodern era of skepticism, we still are all inclined to accept the findings of modern scientific inquiry. Science is based on observation, experimentation, and reasoning. We find comfort in our sure knowledge of facts that are squarely rooted in repeated observation and rational study. But such a scientific view of knowledge has not always been the norm. C. S. Lewis once noted that our view of what we know, and how we know, has changed over the centuries. In the Middle Ages men based their knowledge on the authorities that preceded them. Scholars depended on recognized *auctors*, men who spoke authoritatively of science, ethics, philosophy or theology. If you wanted to know what constituted truth, then you did research and found what was already posited by Aristotle, or Ptolemy, or Galen, or Augustine, or the Bible. But now we think truth must be proved by experiment. We have an entirely different epistemology today.

Or do we?

December 18: THINK ABOUT IT... REALLY!

This returns us to our question. How do we know, really know for certain, that the earth is not the center of the universe? Understand where I am coming from. I have always loved astronomy. As a kid I planned on being an astronomer. I have studied the stars and planets and space since I was a child. I used to have my own telescope, and marveled at the wonders of the moon and other heavenly bodies seen through that magnifying lens. I have read many books on the subject. I have seen the photos of the various bodies in our solar system. I have studied the explanations, and pondered the charts and diagrams of planetary orbits. Through the years I have watched the video images seen on scores, if not hundreds, of programs on PBS, the Discovery Channel, and other TV shows. I have been exposed to all this. And yet... Yet I have never seen the earth orbiting the sun *for myself.* Not once. At no time have I ever been in a position to see the sun at the center of our solar system. I have never observed the earth's rotation from space. I have never watched the planets winging their way through the solar field. I have never seen the Oort Cloud, or observed the path of a comet. Never.

Do I believe these things are real? Yes, indeed I do. But why? Well, let me ask you again. Do *you* believe these things are true? Do you say, "Yes"? Then why? Why do you believe?

Is this not the case: We believe in these things because we have been told they are true? We listened to our science teacher in middle school (or junior high, if you are my age). We paid attention in our physics class in high school. We dutifully heard and believed everything that we were exposed to in all those movies, and books, and TV programs. We know that the earth revolves around the sun, as do the planets, because that is what we have been taught by men and women smarter than we are.

In other words, we believe in the credibility and reliability of certain authorities. Oooops. I thought all that had changed. I thought we no longer believed in *auctors*; that we did not rely on certain *authorities* for our knowledge. That is a medieval concept, not modern, and assuredly not postmodern.

You get my point. We live our lives everyday believing certain things because we have been told they are true. Astronomy is only one example. How many of us have witnessed for ourselves electrical charges going off between the synapses of brain cells? Who has observed the gravitational field of the moon affecting tides? How many people have even witnessed blood actually streaming through arteries and veins? And who among you has seen for yourself an atom, much less an electron or a quark? Is it not true that we believe these things because we have been told they are true?

When I lived in Charlottesville, Va. I used to see a popular bumper sticker. It was probably popular there because C'ville is a university town. And university students (and professors) pride themselves on their doubt. The bumper sticker said, "Question Authority." (I always wanted to stop one of these people and ask them, "Who do you think you are, telling me I have to question authority?") Now I am fairly certain that these people do not live by their own creed. I dare say that they turn their TV's on with full expectation that a continuous stream of electrons is going to light up the screen and provide them with a picture—for they have been told this is what happens. Do you think that if their car won't start, and the mechanic says the ignition switch is bad, that they will replace the radiator? No. Joe the mechanic knows cars much better than they do. And I'd almost be willing to bet (but I won't, because I don't) that if they get sick they will go to a doctor, listen attentively to his advice, take his prescription to the pharmacist, and then swallow the prescribed pills as directed. They don't know if those pills contain antibiotics or arsenic. But they trust the authority of the doctor.

The bottom line is this—we trust authority. We all do. We live by it. We depend on it. Nothing bad about this. It's the way it's supposed to be. But why, why do we balk so much at submitting to the authority of God? Oh, I know. It's called sin. But it's also called foolishness. (Seriously, it is. Read the book of Proverbs.) So when the God of the universe speaks, as He has spoken through His eternal and living word, should we not listen? And (as some assert) is it ignorant or silly for us to heed such authority and accept it by faith? Of course not, especially when we do it ALL the time. We all live by faith in authority. We do so every day of our lives.

So, is the earth the center of the universe? I personally don't think so. But, if you could demonstrate to me that I would have to believe in this fact to be a genuine Bible believer, well... well, I guess I would strangle Copernicus and throw Galileo off the train. You see, I have sense enough to know that I live by submission to authority. As I have said, we all do. The only real question is whose authority are we going to submit to! Aaaah, there's the rub.

Now you may ask, what does this have to with Advent and the upcoming celebration of Christmas? Think about it. So much of the wonder of this season is the result of the amazing story that is the root of all the celebration. This story involves heavenly messengers and angelic announcements, astronomical wonders and fulfilled prophecies, a virginal conception and a miraculous birth, and most of all the divine interruption of history in the Incarnation. Stuff that at face value is hard for many people to swallow. Yet I believe it. I accept it without hesitation or reservation. Why?

Why indeed. I do not have the time, nor would you probably be interested, in learning all of the apologetical reasons that justify having trust and confidence in the Scriptures. But can I tell you this—after years of studying the Bible, reasonable explanations for believing the Bible, other religions and their scriptures, and thinking through this whole matter very carefully, I can say without any doubt that the Bible is trustworthy and true. And even when it speaks of miracles like a supernatural star and a Virgin Birth, I know it can be trusted. It is *the* authority for what I believe, value, and live for. It is an authority we all can reasonably and safely trust.

December 19

O RADIX JESSE

Our calendar is loaded with a wide variety of observances. As just a sampling for December… Did you know that today is Oatmeal Muffin Day? Or that December 5 is Bathtub Party Day. Cotton Candy Day is on December 7. While December 21 is Underdog Day. And on December 15 we celebrate Cat Herder's Day. If all this is confusing to you, just hang on till December 31, which is Make Up Your Mind Day. I have said all this to point out one calendrical observance for today: December 19 is "Look for an Evergreen Day." Yep. You betcha. It sure is.

This is a good day, then, to talk about evergreens and Christmas trees. There is a popular notion that the use of evergreens as Christmas decorations is purely a pagan holdover from pre-Christian Yule and

Saturnalia festivals. Is this true? Well, there is some truth to the matter. Especially as regards some of the evergreens used, especially mistletoe. However, there are a number of evergreens that have a distinctly Christian meaning.

Holly is a prime example. The prickly thorns of the holly tree is a reminder to us of Christ's crown of thorns. That is why in Germany this tree is known as Christdorn, or Christ's thorn. Indeed, there are some legends that holly was actually used in the crown of thorns. According to this legend the berries of the holly were originally white, but they were stained red by Christ's blood, and thus turned red forever. In olden days this plant was considered to have such virtue that it was considered as a holy plant, thus a "holly" or holy tree.

A bit of greenery that is not often used today, but once was very popular, is the rosemary. The name refers to an association with the Virgin Mary. Legend says that on the flight to Egypt the holy family stopped to rest along the way. Herod had sent soldiers in search of the Christ Child. Mary hid the Babe beneath a rosemary bush. Thus, this plant is associated with Mary and Jesus.

Another plant once used more than now is the bay or laurel. Its fragrance is a welcome addition to a cold winter home. It was the plant used for the woven victory crown given to champions in the ancient Greek athletic games. Thus, the bay is a reminder of the victory Christ's coming accomplished for us.

What about the Christmas tree itself? Although the ancient pagans did use evergreen as a part of their yuletide observance, using an entire tree was unknown to them. This custom actually is rather modern, beginning sometime after the Reformation. Tradition credits Martin Luther himself as the originator of the practice. It is said that walking home through a fir forest on a cold Christmas Eve he paused to look at the brilliance of the stars shining in the night sky.

He was awestruck by the sight. When he arrived home he attempted to recreate the sight for his family by placing candles on a small tree he had brought inside. Thus the Christmas tree was born. Whether this legend is true or not, it is a fact that decorating a tree in the manner we do today began sometime in Germany in the 16th century.

What is the significance of the Christmas tree? It has a wealth of imagery for us. It calls to mind the Tree of Life, lost in the Fall but to be restored at the consummation of all things. It reminds us that our Savior died on a tree to pay for our sins. Its evergreen boughs tell us of the eternal life that the Lord has purchased for us. Even the decorations are full of meaning. The star at the top is a reminder of the Magi and the Bethlehem Star. Angels were there to announce His birth. The candy canes evoke memories of the shepherds who heard the message of angels. The lights indicate to us that Christ Himself is the Light of the world. Cookies, gingerbread and other baked items are there because Christ is the Bread of Life. The Christmas balls are decorative orbs that represent Christ as sovereign over the world. All the other trinkets remind us of the joy and blessings that He bestows upon us. Wow! A lot of meaning is packed in just a tree.

During Advent, you might want to consider a very special type of Christmas tree. This is known as a Jesse Tree. It is based on Isaiah 11:1, "A shoot will come up from the stump of Jesse; from his roots a Branch will bear fruit." It was common in Medieval art to picture a reclining man with tree growing up from his body. The man was Jesse, the grandfather of King David. The tree presented the genealogical history of Christ. From this imagery there grew up a custom, once again among German Lutherans, of decorating a tree with symbols of the ancestors of Jesus. Along with this there were also emblems of Old Testament characters, stories, and Messianic prophecies. Often these trees could be very stylized. The custom of a Jesse Tree is not very well known these days. But perhaps we should revive it.

How about setting up a small tree in your home for this purpose. (This would also be good for a church or a Sunday school classroom.) As the season of Advent progresses, place a symbol on this tree. My wife and I used to do this in our church. We used artificial evergreen swags formed into the shape of a Menorah. We decorated with symbols such as these:

An apple for Adam	*A boat for Noah*
A shield of stars for Abraham	*A bundle of sticks for Isaac*
A ladder for Jacob	*A red thread for Rahab*
A sheaf of wheat for Ruth	*A branch for Jesse*
A harp for David	*A crown for Solomon*
A saw for Joseph	*A rose for Mary*

Other symbols could be:

Tablets for Moses	*A scroll for Isaiah*
A fiery wheel for Elijah	*A colorful coat for Joseph*
A tear for Jeremiah	*A trowel for Nehemiah*
A pot shard for Job	*A... well you get the idea.*

It may be a little late to do this now. But what about planning ahead for next year. And then, you do still have a week before Christmas. Maybe you could add these to your Christmas tree. Or set up a display, and add a few symbols each day for the next six days. Whether you actually do this or not, take time to think about the meaning of the Jesse Tree, and the evergreen decorations we use at this time of year. Decorations that remind us of the new life, indeed the eternal life, we have in our Wonderful Savior.

December 20

IGNATIUS OF ANTIOCH

Imagine having John, the son of Zebedee, as your spiritual father and mentor in the faith. Wow! What a privilege. Well, that was the privilege of Ignatius of Antioch, a true hero of the faith remembered on this day.

John apparently trained a number of men for service in the church. Two of the most famous were Polycarp and Ignatius. We know little of Ignatius's early life. However, the 4th century church historian Eusebius tells us that no less a person than Peter himself gave instructions that Ignatius should be appointed as bishop of the church at Antioch. He served in this capacity for 40 years. He is known to have suffered through the persecution of Domitian in the '90's, and guided and led his church well during those difficult times.

Church tradition says that the Emperor Trajan later visited the region, and interrogated Ignatius himself. Ignatius was then condemned to die by Trajan, and ordered to be taken to Rome for his execution. Along the way he was met by crowds of well-wishers. He was known to be such a godly man that he was widely admired. (Indeed, his nickname was Theosphorus, meaning "God-bearer, because he brought the very presence of God with him.) He also was able to visit with his fellow Johannine disciple, Polycarp.

As he traveled to Rome he wrote a series of letters to six churches. These are significant documents for they are among the earliest Christian writings outside the New Testament. They are important for a number of reasons. They quote freely from the New Testament itself. They bear witness to the importance of church structure and worship. And they affirm essential Christian doctrines, such as the Incarnation and Deity of the Lord Jesus.

As we near Christmas, and focus on the birth of Christ, consider some of Ignatius writings about the Savior. Remember, these are from the early years of the second century, only about 85-90 years after Christ's crucifixion and resurrection.

✦ "There is one only Physician, of flesh and of spirit, made and not made, God in man, true Life in death, Son of Mary and Son of God, first passible and then impassible, Jesus Christ our Lord." (Letter to the Ephesians 2:7)

✦ "For our God, Jesus Christ, was according to the dispensation of God conceived in the womb of Mary, of the seed of David, by the Holy Ghost." (Letter to the Ephesians 4:9)

✦ "[Christ] who was truly of the race of David according to the flesh, but the Son of God according to the will and power of God; truly born of the Virgin, and baptized of John, that so all

righteousness might be fulfilled by Him. He was truly crucified by Pontius Pilate and Herod the Tetrach... But I know
that even after His resurrection He was in the flesh; and I
believe that He is still so." (Letter to the Smyrneans 1:4, 5, 9)

✦ "...there is one God who has manifested himself by Jesus
Christ his Son; who is His eternal Word, not coming forth
from silence, who in all things pleased Him that sent Him."
(Letter to the Magnesians 3:2)

Ignatius arrived at Rome on the last day of a series of public
games. He was immediately taken to the Coliseum where the games
were being held. Once thrust into the arena, two lions were released
to attack this aged saint of God. He died quickly under the onslaught
of these beasts. It was on December 20, c. A.D. 117. He apparently
anticipated this end to his life, for on the way to Rome he wrote to the
church there: "I am the wheat of God, and I shall be ground by the
teeth of the wild beasts, that I may be found the pure bread of Christ."
(Letter to the Romans 2:3)

Thinking of Ignatius reminds me of how precious our Christian
faith is. It embodies truths so powerful that men have been willing to
die rather than deny them. Christian doctrine is something that we
must be willing to sacrifice everything for—whether this means to die
for the Gospel, or live everyday in the Gospel.

December 21

THOMAS THE APOSTLE

oday is the traditional day to celebrate the life and martyrdom of Thomas Didymus, one of the Twelve Apostles handpicked by Jesus. When we think of Thomas probably the first thing that comes to mind is that he is known as "Doubting Thomas." It is sad that this great figure of church history is mostly known by one incident in his life. Yes, he questioned the Resurrection of his Lord. But when presented with the most convincing evidence possible, the Lord Jesus Himself in the flesh, then Thomas doubted no longer. He fell to his knees in worship, giving acknowledgement to the divine Being standing before him, "My Lord and my God!" (This is much better than those disciples who saw the resurrected Lord and still doubted, cf. Matthew 28:17.)

We don't really know a lot about Thomas. He is called Didymus, a name meaning "twin." So it is likely he had a twin brother. He is mentioned in several conversations in the Gospels, especially in John. He was certainly present in the Upper Room at Pentecost. He would have been present at the Council of Jerusalem in Acts 15. But after this, he disappears from the biblical record.

However, there is a rich and ancient tradition concerning the missionary work of this Apostle. He is believed to have preached in Syria with great success. Church tradition, and a number of ancient sources, assert that he went on a missionary tour through the Parthian Empire (what is now Iran) and then traveled to India. At first glance this seems a bit far-fetched to many people. But consider some of the evidence for the possible historicity of this tradition.

We do know that there was an enclave of Diaspora Jews living in Kerala in southern India in the first century. We also do know that there was quite a bit of trade between the Romans and the Indian subcontinent. Indeed, there was so much commercial travel going back and forth between the Roman Empire and India that you can see many Roman coins on display in museums in southern India. There is an indigenous church in India that to this day asserts that it was originally founded by the Apostle Thomas himself.

Among the many ancient works that mention Thomas as going to India, one stands out. This is a third century work from Syria called *The Acts of Thomas*. Although apocryphal in nature, it still seems to bear witness to an ancient and legitimate historical tradition. For example, this work tells of Thomas as ministering in two kingdoms in India, one in the north and the other in the south. According to *The Acts* the northern kingdom that Thomas preached in was ruled over by a King Gondophares or Gondaphorus. The entire work was considered purely legendary until fairly recently. In modern times archaeologists have discovered that there was indeed a king by this name ruling in northern India in the late first century. As more evidence is uncovered, the claim that Thomas actually ministered in India seems to be borne out by sound historical and archaeological data.

The end of Thomas' life is also a matter of legend and tradition. The most common legends say that Thomas was skilled as a builder. He hired himself to the Indian king ruling in Mylapore in south India. The king questioned Thomas about his beliefs, but rejected the Gospel. The king then became enraged at Thomas and ordered that he be killed. The Apostle was taken to a hill and stoned. A Brahmin also ran him through with a lance. His death then sparked a general persecution against Christians in the area.

There is a lesson here for us. One mistake on our part does not define our entire lives. Indeed, Thomas the Doubter became Thomas the Believer. He lived a life of such utter devotion to the Resurrected Lord that he traveled thousands of miles proclaiming the Gospel of Christ. His momentary doubt was eclipsed by a life of surrender, service, and sacrifice. His faith has left a legacy that still survives to this day.

WAYS TO COMMEMORATE THOMAS'S DAY

+ In some parts of Britain in bygone days this day was associated with wassailing and mumming. You might want to go Christmas caroling. Or, perhaps improvise an appropriate skit for family and friends. Have a party. Celebrate the season.

+ Pray for India, Iran, the Middle East and other areas where Thomas ministered.

+ Pray for persecuted Christians.

+ Do a study of evidences for the Christian faith.

✦ Examine the evidences for the Resurrection of Christ.

✦ Take time to appreciate the church's rich legacy of architecture.

✦ Visit a large church structure and consider its beauty. How does the art, architecture, design and furnishing of the building inspire you to worship? (The National Cathedral in Washington, D.C. is a great place to visit for this purpose.)

✦ Show your appreciation for those in the building trades. Maybe you could have dinner with a friend who is a carpenter or a mason.

✦ Pray for a missionary, especially native missionaries and the efforts of so many millions to evangelize the world for Christ.

December 22

HE UNDERSTANDS US

Let me say first of all that we really do not know what happened to Joseph. Biblically and historically the adopted father of Jesus disappears from the scene after the incident with adolescent Jesus in the Temple. After this he is only mentioned in passing, such as in speaking of Jesus as the "son of Joseph." What we can assume, and is most likely true, is that Joseph died sometime before Jesus began His public ministry. No other scenario really makes sense. This is what I believe to be the case. With this, then, as a preface, let me tell you a story.

First of all, I must tell you that I am no stranger to dealing with the deaths of loved ones and going to funerals. My mother was one of seven children, and my Dad was one of twelve. Both were among the younger siblings in their respective families. Growing up I experienced the deaths of seemingly multitudes of aunts, uncles, cousins, etc. I lost all of my grandparents by the time I was thirteen. My mother died when I was in high school. To make a long story short, I have had quite a bit of experience with the ol' Grim Reaper.

However, in 1991 an event happened that still stunned me. My father, who had been sick for some time, died on September 24 of that year. He had been in a hospital in Richmond and we were expecting him to die. I remember distinctly, it was a Tuesday afternoon. My older brother (Clinton), my younger sister (Connie) and I all began the time of preparations, grieving, working through the loss. Then early on Thursday morning, just two days later, I received a call from a cousin of mine, a cousin from my mother's side of the family. She told me she was sorry to hear about Clinton's death. I was, of course, very perplexed. I tried to figure out what she meant. The only thing that I could think of was that through my maternal family's grapevine the news of my father's death had reached this cousin. And like playing the kids' game "telephone" or "gossip" the news of the death of my Dad had transformed itself into the death of my brother.

After hanging up the phone, I immediately called my brother's house. His wife answered the phone. I told her, "Colleen, you won't believe the rumor that is circulating around through Mama's family. Someone is saying that Clinton is dead." Colleen's next words froze my heart. I still recall them with precise clarity. "Oh, Victor! I thought you knew. Clinton did die last night. He went to the funeral home to see your Dad. He had a heart attack and died there in the funeral home. I thought you knew because I thought you were there at the funeral home."

As I said earlier, I was stunned. To lose your father is difficult. To lose your father and brother in a space of less than two days is a total shock.

The next few days were a mixed bag. There was sorrow, confusion, disbelief, sadness, and yet joy (both men were now with Jesus!). It was a hard time. But we made it through. The grace of God, a supportive and loving wife, and a sister who can be like a rock were all strengths to me personally.

Over the next few months I continued to work through this shocking experience. Mourning is truly a process and it is not completed in day or a week. (I think we try to rush this journey too often these days. It would be far healthier if we gave people time to work through their grief.) But with God's help, I worked on the process.

Then Christmas comes along. As often happens after such a loss, the holidays were a challenge. I remember that year we were having a Christmas Eve service at our church. It was a beautiful candlelight service—a time of hymns and carols and Scripture readings. I had a small part to play in the early part of the service. After that I sat to one side of the platform, just planning to watch the service. Suddenly my sense of loss, of missing my father and brother, really hit me hard. The congregation was singing carols of joy but my heart was breaking. I tried to focus on worship, but I just felt loneliness and sorrow. It was a miserable feeling.

Then—the Lord spoke to me. No, it was not an audible voice. No thunder, no lightning. But it was one of those times when you know that you know that you know you are hearing a direct word from God. It might not be an audible sound, but it booms its way into your heart. You know God is speaking. Do you comprehend what I mean? If you have ever experienced this, then you understand.

Anyway, as I said, the Lord spoke to me. I knew it was Jesus. And in the midst of my hurt and pain, I heard Him say so simply and so distinctly, "*Son, remember... I lost my father too.*"

Wow! What a thunderbolt! Jesus understands. He knows what I am feeling. He has been here. He has lived through this. He has experienced the pain and loss of losing a loved one. He who existed (and exists) in eternity with the heavenly Father has also known the pain of standing at the grave of His earthly father. He knows!

What a comfort to my soul. Tears flooded my eyes—tears that had changed from an expression of grief to a sense of gratitude, acknowledgement, help, being cared for. Jesus knows and understands. With this word from the Lord my whole outlook was transformed.

This is what I want to share with you today: Jesus understands where you are and He comes to help you in your time of need.

And, can I tell you, this is the message of Advent and Christmas. He came here. He pitched His tent among us. He became one of us. He lived here as a man, as True Man. He was a real, true human being. He did this for our salvation. Yes, that is true. But He also did this for our succor. "O tidings of comfort and joy!"

> *"Because God's children are human beings—made of flesh and blood—the Son also became flesh and blood... We also know that the Son did not come to help angels; he came to help the descendants of Abraham. Therefore, it was necessary for him to be made in every respect like us, his brothers and sisters, so that he could be our merciful and faithful High Priest before God. Then he could offer a sacrifice that would take away the sins of the people. Since he himself has gone through suffering and testing, he is able to help us when we are being tested."*
>
> ~Hebrews 2:14a, 16-18

December 23

A GOODLY HERITAGE?

In some church traditions this is the day to remember the ancestors of Christ. Ever think about these people? It is definitely a motley crew. You have the good, the bad, the ugly, and the just plain weird. Indeed, I think a case could be made for the genealogy of Christ being an apologetic for the genuineness of the New Testament. If you were going to make up a story about a mythical Savior, and create a list of His ancestors, wouldn't you have His progenitors be heroes, men of great moral courage, women of virtue, people who were noble and exemplary in character? But that is not what you get in the Gospels. It doesn't seem to be the kind of list that somebody would just make up out of their imagination. Nobody's that honest.

Take a look at the genealogy in Matthew 1. You start with Abraham, a man who fudged on the truth and got ahead of God's plan when it came to having children. Then you have Jacob, a man noted for deception and trickery. Judah had a liaison with a woman he thought was a prostitute, not knowing it was actually his own daughter-in-law. Boaz married Rahab, who was a professional "lady of the evening." Their son, Boaz, married a foreign, pagan woman. Their grandson was the great King David. Great? Yes. But also an adulterer and murderer.

Let's not stop here. David's son was the mighty King Solomon, noted for his glory and wisdom. But also noted for marrying 100's of women, building altars to foreign gods, and engaging in idolatry. There follows a list of kings, good and bad, and some who were both. For example, Asa, who started out as a righteous ruler, but ended up compromising his faith, and displaying disloyalty to God. Drop down the list a little further to Asa's grandson, Jehoram. He married into the family of Ahab, and incited Judah to idolatry again. He murdered his brothers, as well. A few more kings, good and bad, and you come to Manasseh, the most wicked king in the history of Judah, the southern kingdom. He sacrificed his children to pagan gods. He practiced sorcery and magic. He filled Jerusalem with bloodshed. He worshipped stars, sun, moon and heathen demonic gods. Quite a man, huh? And yet, another ancestor of Jesus!

After Manasseh, you have his son, Amon, who was completely given over to idolatry and wickedness. Things temporarily get better with Josiah. But after his death there is a succession of his sons and grandsons who rule, as things get worse and worse in Judah. These kings are so wicked, and the kingdom so corrupt that God finally gets totally fed up, and sends them into exile. There seems to be nothing left for the house of David but judgment...

But it's really not judgment alone; for there is a promise, a promise of God for the House of David. A promise of an eternal reign of a truly righteous King. A promise fulfilled in Jesus Himself.

There are some valuable lessons for us here, considering this heritage of the Messiah. First of all, your ancestors, your family legacy, does not determine who you are. You can rise above your roots, your predecessors. As I heard someone once observe, "Your past is not a blueprint for your future!" Don't feel trapped by your heritage. Christ didn't have such a great family tree, and He is the Son of God. Secondly, there is always hope in the providence and sovereignty of God. God can take any situation, any set of happenings, any group of people, no matter how seemingly hopeless, and turn it to good. Jesus came from a line of liars, murderers, adulterers, and idolaters. Yet that did not prevent Him from being the Chosen One of God. Truly where sin does abound, grace does much more abound (Romans 5:20). God's power and love and mercy are bigger and greater than any sin, or any sinner.

During this Advent season, you have been encouraged to examine yourself, to mourn for your sin, and to repent of wrong in your life. And this is good. But do not let an awareness of your struggles with your failings bog you down in life. God is greater than your struggles. Jesus is bigger than your sin. There is nothing that can limit or hinder what God wants to do in your life, even your own sin—if you confess and bring it to Him. His grace is that big, and that good.

Don't let where you have come from determine where you are going. Jesus has shown the way to better things, for each of us.

December 24

HIS APPEARING

"Finally, there is laid up for me the crown of righteousness, which the Lord, the righteous Judge, will give to me on that Day, and not to me only but also to all have loved His appearing." 2 Timothy 4:8

As we have mentioned previously, one of the themes of Advent is the coming of the Lord. Indeed, the word Advent means "coming." During this season we relive the journey to Christmas. We remind ourselves what it was like before Christ came. We remember the words of the prophets, the hopes of Israel, the dreams of a coming Messiah. We sense once again the anticipation, the longing for the Savior.

And we prepare ourselves to rejoice—for He did come. And when He came, He completely and fully completed the task God had planned for Him. He did what He did "that the Scriptures might be fulfilled." Indeed, in His coming He fulfilled over 300 specific prophecies. Imagine that! Prophecies about His birth, who would visit Him as an infant, His hometown, His life, His ministry, His Passion, His death and resurrection. All outlined in vivid and amazing detail. How marvelous!

Yet there is something that is even more marvelous, as hard as that is to believe. For the Scriptures not only have 300 prophecies about His first coming, but there are thousands of verses that point to His Second Coming. Think of all those promises of the coming Kingdom, the reign of peace and righteousness. Think of all those warnings about the terrible and awesome Day of the Lord. Think of the glories of His restoration and renewal of all things—including the heavens and the earth themselves. When we read through the Bible, Old and New Covenants, we see the promise of His Return as a consistent and constant theme.

Along with the rest of the early church, Paul looked forward to this future event. In fact, Paul made it evident that he _loved_ the promise of Christ's appearing. This gives me pause. Do _I_ love His appearing? Do I long to see Him? The people of God before His first coming had a great desire, a deeply felt anticipation for the coming of Messiah. Do I have a desire just as deep and just as dearly felt as they? Do I eagerly await His coming?

I am concerned about this, for myself and for the church in general. I am afraid that we may have become so settled here that we think this is our home. We are so comfortable in this world, this life, that we no longer yearn for another, a better life, a far better home. Are we so satisfied with our present condition that our hearts no longer beat faster at the promise of His appearing? Is the Bride so in love with her Bridegroom that she counts the days, the minutes, the seconds until He comes for her?

I cannot answer for you. I can only answer for myself.

And my answer is this: As we conclude this season of Advent, as we remember His first coming, we must ask God to put in our hearts a renewed desire for His Second Advent. Lord, may this season not only bring us the joy of knowing the Savior has come—but also a rekindled passion to see the Lord come again. Father, may we pray with fresh fervor: "Thy kingdom come!"

"Even so, come Lord Jesus!"

Revelation 22:20

The Ministry
OF ANM

ANM Publications is a ministry initiative of
Advancing Native Missions

Advancing Native Missions (ANM) is a U.S.-based Christian missions agency. However, unlike many such agencies that are involved in sending missionaries from America to other places around the world, ANM works with indigenous missionaries. Indigenous (or native) missionaries are Christian workers who minister within their own sphere of influence proclaiming the Gospel of Jesus Christ to their own people. ANM then works to connect Christians in America with these brothers and sisters, to equip and encourage them. Our goal is to build relationships of love and trust between indigenous missionaries and North American individuals and churches. In this way, the entire body of Christ becomes involved in completing the Great Commission. **"And this gospel of the kingdom shall be preached in all the world as a witness to all nations, and then the end shall come"** (Matthew 24:14).

If you would like to know how you can become an effective coworker with native missionaries to reach the unreached for Jesus Christ, contact ANM at requests@adnamis.org, call us at 540-456-7111, or visit our website: www.AdvancingNativeMissions.com.